ABC of Reading

ABC of Reading

by

EZRA POUND

FABER AND FABER
London · Boston

First published in 1951
by Faber and Faber Limited
3 Queen Square London W.C.1
First published in this edition 1961
Reprinted 1963, 1968, 1973 and 1979
Printed in Great Britain by
Whitstable Litho Ltd., Whitstable, Kent
All rights reserved

ISBN 0 571 05892 2

Contents

2

A B C

Or gradus ad Parnassum, for those who might like to learn. The book is not addressed to those who have arrived at full knowledge of the subject without knowing the facts

How to Study Poetry

THE present book is intended to meet the need for fuller and simpler explanation of the method outlined in *How to Read*. *How to Read* may be considered as a controversial pamphlet summarizing the more active or spiky parts of the author's earlier critical skirmishing, and taking count of an enemy. The present pages should be impersonal enough to serve as a text-book. The author hopes to follow the tradition of Gaston Paris and S. Reinach, that is, to produce a text-book that can also be read 'for pleasure as well as profit' by those no longer in school; by those who have not been to school; or by those who in their college days suffered those things which most of my own generation suffered.

A private word to teachers and professors will be found toward the end of the volume. I am not idly sowing thorns in their path. I should like to make even their lot and life more exhilarating and to save even them from unnecessary boredom in class-room.

Warning

1 There is a longish dull stretch shortly after the beginning of the book. The student will have to endure it. I am at that place trying by all means to avoid ambiguity, in the hope of saving the student's time later.

2 Gloom and solemnity are entirely out of place in even the most rigorous study of an art originally intended to make glad the heart of man.

> Gravity, a mysterious carriage of the
> body to conceal the defects of the mind.
>
> LAURENCE STERNE

3 The harsh treatment here accorded a number of meritorious writers is not aimless, but proceeds from a firm conviction that the only way to keep the best writing in circulation, or to 'make the best poetry popular', is by drastic separation of the best from a great mass of writing that has been long considered of value, that has overweighted all curricula, and that is to be blamed for the very pernicious current idea that a good book must be of necessity a dull one.

A classic is classic not because it conforms to certain structural rules, or fits certain definitions (of which its author had quite probably never heard). It is classic because of a certain eternal and irrepressible freshness.

An Italian state examiner, jolted by my edition of Cavalcanti, expressed admiration at the almost ultra-modernity of Guido's language.

Ignorant men of genius are constantly rediscovering 'laws' of art which the academics had mislaid or hidden.

The author's conviction on this day of New Year is that music begins to atrophy when it departs too far from the dance; that poetry begins to atrophy when it gets too far from music; but this must not be taken as implying that all good music is dance music or all poetry lyric. Bach and Mozart are never too far from physical movement.

> Nunc est bibendum
> Nunc pede libero
> Pulsanda tellus.

SECTION ONE

Chapter One

1

We live in an age of science and of abundance. The care and reverence for books as such, proper to an age when no book was duplicated until someone took the pains to copy it out by hand, is obviously no longer suited to 'the needs of society', or to the conservation of learning. The weeder is supremely needed if the Garden of the Muses is to persist as a garden.

The proper METHOD for studying poetry and good letters is the method of contemporary biologists, that is careful first-hand examination of the matter, and continual COMPARISON of one 'slide' or specimen with another.

No man is equipped for modern thinking until he has understood the anecdote of Agassiz and the fish:

A post-graduate student equipped with honours and diplomas went to Agassiz to receive the final and finishing touches. The great man offered him a small fish and told him to describe it.

Post-Graduate Student: 'That's only a sunfish.'

Agassiz: 'I know that. Write a description of it.'

After a few minutes the student returned with the description of the Ichthus Heliodiplodokus, or whatever term is used to conceal the common sunfish from vulgar knowledge, family of Heliichtherinkus, etc., as found in textbooks of the subject.

Agassiz again told the student to describe the fish.

The student produced a four-page essay. Agassiz then told him to look at the fish. At the end of three weeks the fish was in an advanced state of decomposition. but the student knew something about it.

By this method modern science has arisen, not on the narrow edge of mediaeval logic suspended in a vacuum.

'Science does not consist in inventing a number of more or less abstract entities corresponding to the number of things you wish to find out', says a French commentator on Einstein. I don't know whether that clumsy translation of a long French sentence is clear to the general reader.

The first definite assertion of the applicability of scientific method to literary criticism is found in Ernest Fenollosa's *Essay on the Chinese Written Character*.

The complete despicability of official philosophic thought, and, if the reader will really think carefully of what I am trying to tell him, the most stinging insult and at the same time convincing proof of the general nullity and incompetence of organized intellectual life in America, England, their universities in general, and their learned publications at large, could be indicated by a narrative of the difficulties I encountered in getting Fenollosa's essay printed at all.

A text-book is no place for anything that could be interpreted or even misinterpreted as a personal grievance.

Let us say that the editorial minds, and those of men in power in the literary and educational bureaucracy for the fifty years preceding 1934, have not always differed very greatly from that of the tailor Blodgett who prophesied that: 'sewing machines will never come into general use'.

Fenollosa's essay was perhaps too far ahead of his time to be easily comprehended. He did not proclaim his method as a method. He was trying to explain the Chinese ideograph as a means of transmission and registration of thought. He got to the root of the matter, to the root of the difference between what is valid in Chinese thinking and invalid or misleading in a great deal of European thinking and language.

The simplest statement I can make of his meaning is as follows:

In Europe, if you ask a man to define anything, his definition always moves away from the simple things that he knows perfectly well, it recedes into an unknown region, that is a region of remoter and progressively remoter abstraction.

Thus if you ask him what red is, he says it is a 'colour'.

If you ask him what a colour is, he tells you it is a vibration or a refraction of light, or a division of the spectrum.

And if you ask him what vibration is, he tells you it is a mode of energy, or something of that sort, until you arrive at a modality of being, or non-being, or at any rate you get in beyond your depth, and beyond his depth.

In the middle ages when there wasn't any material science, as we now understand it, when human knowledge could not make automobiles run, or electricity carry language through the air, etc., etc., in short, when learning consisted in little more than splitting up of terminology, there was a good deal of care for terminology, and the general exactitude in the use of abstract terms may have been (probably was) higher.

I mean a mediaeval theologian took care not to define a dog in terms that would have applied just as well to a dog's tooth or its hide, or the noise it makes when lapping water; but all your teachers will tell you that science developed more rapidly after Bacon had suggested the direct examination of phenomena, and after Galileo and others had stopped discussing things so much, and had begun really to look at them, and to invent means (like the telescope) of seeing them better.

The most useful living member of the Huxley family has emphasized the fact that the telescope wasn't merely an idea, but that it was very definitely a technical achievement.

By contrast to the method of abstraction, or of defining things in more and still more general terms, Fenollosa emphasizes the method of science, 'which is the method of poetry', as distinct from that of 'philosophic discussion', and is the way the Chinese go about it in their ideograph or abbreviated picture writing.

To go back to the beginning of history, you probably know that there is spoken language and written language, and that there are two kinds of written language, one based on sound and the other on sight.

You speak to an animal with a few simple noises and

gestures. Levy-Bruhl's account of primitive languages in Africa records languages that are still bound up with mimicry and gesture.

The Egyptians finally used abbreviated pictures to represent sounds, but the Chinese still use abbreviated pictures AS pictures, that is to say, Chinese ideogram does not try to be the picture of a sound, or to be a written sign recalling a sound, but it is still the picture of a thing; of a thing in a given position or relation, or of a combination of things. It *means* the thing or the action or situation, or quality germane to the several things that it pictures.

Gaudier Brzeska, who was accustomed to looking at the real shape of things, could read a certain amount of Chinese writing without ANY STUDY. He said, 'Of course, you can *see* it's a horse' (or a wing or whatever).

In tables showing primitive Chinese characters in one column and the present 'conventionalized' signs in another, anyone can see how the ideogram for man or tree or sunrise developed, or 'was simplified from', or was reduced to the essentials of the first picture of man, tree or sunrise.

Thus

人　　man

木　　tree

日　　sun

東　　sun tangled in the tree's branches, as
　　　　at sunrise, meaning now the East.

But when the Chinaman wanted to make a picture of

21

something more complicated, or of a general idea, how did he go about it?

He is to define red. How can he do it in a picture that isn't painted in red paint?

He puts (or his ancestor put) together the abbreviated pictures of

ROSE   CHERRY

IRON RUST   FLAMINGO

That, you see, is very much the kind of thing a biologist does (in a very much more complicated way) when he gets together a few hundred or thousand slides, and picks out what is necessary for his general statement. Something that fits the case, that applies in all of the cases.

The Chinese 'word' or ideogram for red is based on something everyone KNOWS.

(If ideogram had developed in England, the writers would possibly have substituted the front side of a robin, or something less exotic than a flamingo.)

Fenollosa was telling how and why a language written in this way simply HAD TO STAY POETIC; simply couldn't help being and staying poetic in a way that a column of English type might very well not stay poetic.

He died before getting round to publishing and proclaiming a 'method'.

This is nevertheless the RIGHT WAY to study poetry, or literature, or painting. It is in fact the way the more intelligent members of the general public DO study painting. If you want to find out something about painting you go to the National Gallery, or the Salon Carré, or the Brera, or the Prado, and LOOK at the pictures.

For every reader of books on art, 1,000 people go to LOOK at the paintings. Thank heaven!

LABORATORY CONDITIONS

A SERIES of coincidences has permitted me (1933) to demonstrate the *How to Read* thesis in a medium nearer to poetry than painting is. A group of serious musicians (Gerart Münch, Olga Rudge, Luigi Sansoni), a town hall at our disposition (Rapallo), we presented among other things the following programmes:

Oct. 10.

From the Chilesotti MSS. Münch transcription: Francesco da Milano: 'Canzone degli Uccelli', recast from Janequin.

Giovanni Terzi: Suite di Ballo.

Corelli: Sonata in La maj., two violins and piano.

J. S. Bach. Sonata in Do maj.   ditto.

Debussy: Sonata per piano e violino.

Dec. 5.

Collezione Chilesotti: Severi: due Arie.

Roncalli: Preludio,

Gigua, Passacaglia.

Bach: Toccata (piano solo, ed. Busoni).
Bach: Concerto Re maj. for two violins and piano.
Ravel: Sonata per violino e pianoforte.

There was nothing fortuitous. The point of this experiment is that everyone present at the two concerts now knows a great deal more about the relations, the relative weight, etc., of Debussy and Ravel than they possibly could have found out by reading ALL the criticisms that have ever been written of both.

The best volume of musical criticism I have ever encountered is Boris De Schloezer's *Stravinsky*. What do I know after reading it that I didn't know before?

I am aware of De Schloezer's mental coherence, and thoroughness. I am delighted by one sentence, possibly the only one in the book that I remember (approximately): 'Melody is the most artificial thing in music', meaning that it is furthest removed from anything the composer finds THERE, ready in nature, needing only direct imitation or copying. It is therefore the root, the test, etc.

This is an aphorism, a general statement. For me it is profoundly true. It *can* be used as a measuring-rod to Stravinsky or any other composer. BUT for actual knowledge of Stravinsky? Where De Schloezer refers to works I have heard, I get most, perhaps all, of his meaning.

Where he refers to works I have not heard, I get his 'general idea' but I acquire no real knowledge.

My final impression is that he was given a rather poor case, that he has done his best for his client, and ultimately left Stravinsky flat on his back, although he has explained

24

why the composer went wrong, or couldn't very well have
done otherwise.

2

ANY general statement is like a cheque drawn on a bank.
Its value depends on what is there to meet it. If Mr.
Rockefeller draws a cheque for a million dollars it is good.
If I draw one for a million it is a joke, a hoax, it has no
value. If it is taken seriously, the writing of it becomes a
criminal act.

The same applies with cheques against knowledge. If
Marconi says something about ultra-short waves it MEANS
something. Its meaning can only be properly estimated by
someone who KNOWS.

You do not accept a stranger's cheques without reference.
In writing, a man's 'name' is his reference. He has, after a
time, credit. It may be sound, it may be like the late Mr.
Kreuger's.

The verbal manifestation on any bank cheque is very
much like that on any other.

Your cheque, if good, means ultimately delivery of
something you want.

An abstract or general statement is GOOD if it be
ultimately found to correspond with the facts.

BUT no layman can tell at sight whether it is good or
bad.

Hence (omitting various intermediate steps) . . . hence the almost stationary condition of knowledge throughout the middle ages. Abstract arguments didn't get mankind rapidly forward, or rapidly extend the borders of knowledge.

THE IDEOGRAMMIC METHOD OR THE METHOD OF SCIENCE

HANG a painting by Carlo Dolci beside a Cosimo Tura. You cannot prevent Mr. Buggins from preferring the former, but you can very seriously impede his setting up a false tradition of teaching on the assumption that Tura has never existed, or that the qualities of the Tura are non-existent or outside the scope of the possible.

A general statement is valuable only in REFERENCE to the known objects or facts.

Even if the general statement of an ignorant man is 'true', it leaves his mouth or pen without any great validity. He doesn't KNOW what he is saying. That is, he doesn't know it or mean it in anything like the degree that a man of experience would or does. Thus a very young man can be quite 'right' without carrying conviction to an older man who is wrong and who may quite well be wrong and still know a good deal that the younger man doesn't know.

One of the pleasures of middle age is to *find out* that one WAS right, and that one was much righter than one knew at say seventeen or twenty-three.

. . . . .

26

This doesn't in the least rule out the uses of logic, or of good guesses, or of intuitions and total perceptions, or of 'seeing how the thing HAD TO BE'.

It has, however, a good deal to do with the efficiency of verbal manifestation, and with the transmittiability of a conviction.

Chapter Two

What *is literature, what is language, etc.*??

Literature is language charged with meaning.

'Great literature is simply language charged with meaning to the utmost possible degree' (E. P. in *How to Read*).

But language?

Spoken or written?

Spoken language is noise divided up into a system of grunts, hisses, etc. They call it 'articulate' speech.

'Articulate' means that it is zoned, and that a number of people are agreed on the categories.

That is to say, we have a more or less approximate agreement about the different noises represented by

a, b, c, d, etc.

Written language, as I said in the opening chapter, can consist (as in Europe, etc.) of signs representing these various noises.

There is a more or less approximate agreement that groups of these noises or signs shall more or less correspond with some object, action or condition.

cat, motion, pink.

The other kind of language starts by being a picture of

the cat, or of something moving, or being, or of a group of things which occur under certain circumstances, or which participate a common quality.

APPROACH

IT doesn't, in our contemporary world, so much matter where you begin the examination of a subject, so long as you keep on until you get round again to your starting-point. As it were, you start on a sphere, or a cube; you must keep on until you have seen it from all sides. Or if you think of your subject as a stool or table, you must keep on until it has three legs and will stand up, or four legs and won't tip over too easily.

WHAT is the USE OF LANGUAGE? WHY STUDY LITERATURE?

LANGUAGE was obviously created, and is, obviously, USED for communication.

'Literature is news that STAYS news.'

These things are matters of degree. Your communication can be more or less exact. The INTEREST in a statement can be more or less durable.

I cannot for example, wear out my interest in the *Ta Hio* of Confucius, or in the Homeric poems.

It is very difficult to read the same detective story twice. Or let us say, only a very good 'tec' will stand re-reading, after a very long interval, and because one has paid so

29

little attention to it that one has almost completely forgotten it.

The above are natural phenomena, they serve as measuring-rods, or instruments. For no two people are these 'measures' identical.

The critic who doesn't make a personal statement, *in re* measurements he himself has made, is merely an unreliable critic. He is not a measurer but a repeater of other men's results.

KRINO, to pick out for oneself,   to choose. That's what the word means.

No one would be foolish enough to ask me to pick out a horse or even an automobile for him.

Pisanello painted horses so that one remembers the painting, and the Duke of Milan sent him to Bologna to BUY horses.

Why a similar kind of 'horse sense' can't be applied in the study of literature is, and has always been, beyond my comprehension.

Pisanello had to LOOK at the horses.

You would think that anyone wanting to know about poetry would do one of two things or both. I.E., LOOK AT it or listen to it. He might even think about it?

And if he wanted advice he would go to someone who KNEW something about it.

If you wanted to know something about an automobile, would you go to a man who had made one and driven it, or to a man who had merely heard about it?

And of two men who had made automobiles, would you go to one who had made a good one, or one who had made a botch?

Would you look at the actual car or only at the specifications?

In the case of poetry, there is, or seems to be, a good deal to be looked at. And there seem to be very few authentic specifications available.

Dante says: 'A canzone is a composition of words set to music.'

I don't know any better point to start from.

Coleridge or De Quincey said that the quality of a 'great poet is everywhere present, and nowhere visible as a distinct excitement', or something of that sort.
This would be a more dangerous *starting*-point. It is probably true.
Dante's statement is the better place to begin because it starts the reader or hearer from what he actually sees or hears, instead of distracting his mind from that actuality to something which can only be approximately deduced or conjectured FROM the actuality, and for which the *evidence* can be nothing save the particular and limited extent of the actuality.

Chapter Three

1

Literature does not exist in a vacuum. Writers as such have a definite social function exactly proportioned to their ability AS WRITERS. This is their main use. All other uses are relative, and temporary, and can be estimated only in relation to the views of a particular estimator.

Partisans of particular ideas may value writers who agree with them more than writers who do not, they may, and often do, value bad writers of their own party or religion more than good writers of another party or church.

But there is one basis susceptible of estimation and independent of all questions of viewpoint.

Good writers are those who keep the language efficient. That is to say, keep it accurate, keep it clear. It doesn't matter whether the good writer wants to be useful, or whether the bad writer wants to do harm.

Language is the main means of human communication. If an animal's nervous system does not transmit sensations and stimuli, the animal atrophies.

If a nation's literature declines, the nation atrophies and decays.

Your legislator can't legislate for the public good, your commander can't command, your populace (if you be a democratic country) can't instruct its 'representatives', save by language.

The fogged language of swindling classes serves only a temporary purpose.

A limited amount of communication *in re* special subjects, passes via mathematical formulae, via the plastic arts, via diagrams, via purely musical forms, but no one proposes substituting these for the common speech, nor does anyone suggest that it would be either possible or advisable.

UBICUNQUE LINGUA ROMANA, IBI ROMA

GREECE and Rome civilized BY LANGUAGE. Your language is in the care of your writers.

['Insults o'er dull and speechless tribes']

but this language is not merely for records of great things done. Horace and Shakespeare can proclaim its monumental and mnemonic value, but that doesn't exhaust the matter.

Rome rose with the idiom of Caesar, Ovid, and Tacitus, she declined in a welter of rhetoric, the diplomat's 'language to conceal thought', and so forth.

The man of understanding can no more sit quiet and resigned while his country lets its literature decay, and lets good writing meet with contempt, than a good doctor could sit quiet and contented while some ignorant child was infecting itself with tuberculosis under the impression that it was merely eating jam tarts.

.   .   .   .   .

33

It is very difficult to make people understand the *impersonal* indignation that a decay of writing can cause men who understand what it implies, and the end whereto it leads. It is almost impossible to express any degree of such indignation without being called 'embittered', or something of that sort.

Nevertheless the 'statesman cannot govern, the scientist cannot participate his discoveries, men cannot agree on wise action without language', and all their deeds and conditions are affected by the defects or virtues of idiom.

A people that grows accustomed to sloppy writing is a people in process of losing grip on its empire and on itself. And this looseness and blowsiness is not anything as simple and scandalous as abrupt and disordered syntax.

It concerns the relation of expression to meaning. Abrupt and disordered syntax can be at times very honest, and an elaborately constructed sentence can be at times merely an elaborate camouflage.

2

THE sum of human wisdom is not contained in any one language, and no single language is CAPABLE of expressing all forms and degrees of human comprehension.

This is a very unpalatable and bitter doctrine. But I cannot omit it.

People occasionally develop almost a fanaticism in combating the ideas 'fixed' in a single language. These are generally speaking 'the prejudices of the nation' (any nation).

Different climates and different bloods have different needs, different spontaneities, different reluctances, different ratios between different groups of impulse and unwillingness, different constructions of throat, and all these leave trace in the language, and leave it more ready and more unready for certain communications and registrations.

THE READER'S AMBITION may be mediocre, and the ambitions of no two readers will be identical. The teacher can only aim his instruction at those who most *want* to learn, but he can at any rate start them with an 'appetizer', he can at least hand them a printed list of the things to be learned in literature, or in a given section thereof.

The first bog of inertia may be simple ignorance of the extent of the subject, or a simple unwillingness to move away from one area of semi-ignorance. The greatest barrier is probably set up by teachers who know a little more than the public, who want to exploit their fractional knowledge, and who are thoroughly opposed to making the least effort to learn anything more.

Chapter Four

1

'Great literature is simply language charged with meaning
to the utmost possible degree.'

Dichten = condensare.

I begin with poetry because it is the most concentrated
form of verbal expression. Basil Bunting, fumbling about
with a German-Italian dictionary, found that this idea of
poetry as concentration is as old almost as the German
language. 'Dichten' is the German verb corresponding to
the noun 'Dichtung' meaning poetry, and the lexicographer has rendered it by the Italian verb meaning 'to
condense'.

The charging of language is done in three principal ways:
You receive the language as your race has left it, the words
have meanings which have 'grown into the race's skin';
the Germans say 'wie in den Schnabel gewachsen', as it
grows in his beak. And the good writer chooses his words
for their 'meaning', but that meaning is not a set, cut-off
thing like the move of knight or pawn on a chess-board.
It comes up with roots, with associations, with how and
where the word is familiarly used, or where it has been
used brilliantly or memorably.

36

You can hardly say 'incarnadine' without one or more of your auditors thinking of a particular line of verse.

Numerals and words referring to human inventions have hard, cut-off meanings. That is, meanings which are more obtrusive than a word's 'associations'.

Bicycle now has a cut-off meaning.

But tandem, or 'bicycle built for two', will probably throw the image of a past decade upon the reader's mental screen.

There is no end to the number of qualities which some people can associate with a given word or kind of word, and most of these vary with the individual.

You have to go almost exclusively to Dante's criticism to find a set of OBJECTIVE categories for words. Dante called words 'buttered' and 'shaggy' because of the different NOISES they make. Or *pexa et hirsuta*, combed and hairy.

He also divided them by their different associations.

NEVERTHELESS you still charge words with meaning mainly in three ways, called phanopoeia, melopoeia, logopoeia. You use a word to throw a visual image on to the reader's imagination, or you charge it by sound, or you use groups of words to do this.

Thirdly, you take the greater risk of using the word in some special relation to 'usage', that is, to the kind of context in which the reader expects, or is accustomed, to find it.

37

This is the last means to develop, it can only be used by the sophisticated.

(If you want really to understand what I am talking about, you will have to read, ultimately, Propertius and Jules Laforgue.)

IF YOU WERE STUDYING CHEMISTRY you would be told that there are a certain number of elements, a certain number of more usual chemicals, chemicals most in use, or easiest to find. And for the sake of clarity in your experiments, you would probably be given these substances 'pure' or as pure as you could conveniently get them.

IF YOU WERE A CONTEMPORARY book-keeper you would probably use the loose-leaf system, by which business houses separate archives from facts that are in use, or that are likely to be frequently needed for reference.

Similar conveniences are possible in the study of literature.

Any amateur of painting knows that modern galleries lay great stress on 'good hanging', that is, of putting important pictures where they can be well seen, and where the eye will not be confused, or the feet wearied by searching for the masterpiece on a vast expanse of wall cumbered with rubbish.

At this point I can't very well avoid printing a set of categories that considerably antedate my own *How to Read*.

2

WHEN you start searching for 'pure elements' in literature you will find that literature has been created by the following classes of persons:

1   Inventors. Men who found a new process, or whose extant work gives us the first known example of a process.

2   The masters. Men who combined a number of such processes, and who used them as well as or better than the inventors.

3   The diluters. Men who came after the first two kinds of writer, and couldn't do the job quite as well.

4   Good writers without salient qualities. Men who are fortunate enough to be born when the literature of a given country is in good working order, or when some particular branch of writing is 'healthy'. For example, men who wrote sonnets in Dante's time, men who wrote short lyrics in Shakespeare's time or for several decades thereafter, or who wrote French novels and stories after Flaubert had shown them how.

5   Writers of belles-lettres. That is, men who didn't really invent anything, but who specialized in some parti-

cular part of writing, who couldn't be considered as 'great men' or as authors who were trying to give a complete presentation of life, or of their epoch.

6 The starters of crazes.

Until the reader knows the first two categories he will never be able 'to see the wood for the trees'. He may know what he 'likes'. He may be a 'compleat book-lover', with a large library of beautifully printed books, bound in the most luxurious bindings, but he will never be able to sort out what he knows or to estimate the value of one book in relation to others, and he will be more confused and even less able to make up his mind about a book where a new author is 'breaking with convention' than to form an opinion about a book eighty or a hundred years old.

He will never understand why a specialist is annoyed with him for trotting out a second- or third-hand opinion about the merits of his favourite bad writer.

Until you have made your own survey and your own closer inspection you might at least beware and avoid accepting opinions:

1 From men who haven't themselves produced notable work (vide p. 17).

2 From men who have not themselves taken the risk of printing the results of their own personal inspection and survey, even if they are seriously making one.

3

COMPASS, SEXTANT, OR LAND MARKS

LET the student brace himself and prepare for the worst. I am coming to my list of the minimum that a man would have to read if he hoped to know what a given new book was worth. I mean as he would know whether a given pole-vault was remarkably high, or a given tennis player at all likely to play in a Davis Cup match.

You might think it would be safe to print such a list, or that it 'would be the last thing a reader could misunderstand'. But there would seem to be almost no limit to what people can and will misunderstand when they are not doing their utmost to get at a writer's meaning.

With regard to the following list, one ingenious or ingenuous attacker suggested that I had included certain poems in this list because I had myself translated them. The idea that during twenty-five years' search I had translated the poems BECAUSE they were the key positions or the best illustrations, seems not to have occurred to him. He surpassed himself by suggesting that the poem of Bion's was an afterthought mentioned out of place, and that I had mistaken it for a poem of Moschus which he himself had translated. That is what comes of trying to bore people as little as possible, and to put down one's matter in the least possible space.

The Bion is separated by centuries from the Homer and Sappho. In studying the earlier parts of the list, the attention would, I think, have gone to the WRITING, to the narrative, to the clarity of expression, but would not have naturally focused itself on the melodic devices, on the fitting of the words, their SOUND and ultimately their meaning, to the tune.

The Bion is put with those troubadours for the sake of contrast, and in order to prevent the reader from thinking that one set or a half-dozen sets of melodic devices constituted the whole of that subject.

AT ABOUT THIS POINT the weak-hearted reader usually sits down in the road, removes his shoes and weeps that he 'is a bad linguist' or that he or she can't possibly learn all those languages.

One has to divide the readers who want to be experts from those who do not, and divide, as it were, those who want to see the world from those who merely want to know WHAT PART OF IT THEY LIVE IN.

When it comes to the question of poetry, a great many people don't even want to know that their own country does not occupy ALL the available surface of the planet. The idea seems in some way to insult them.

Nevertheless the maximum of **phanopoeia** [throwing a visual image on the mind] is probably reached by the Chinese, due in part to their particular kind of written language.

In the languages known to me (which do not include Persian and Arabic) the maximum of **melopoeia** is reached in Greek, with certain developments in Provençal which are not in Greek, and which are of a different KIND than the Greek.

And it is my firm conviction that a man can learn more about poetry by really knowing and examining a few of the best poems than by meandering about among a great many. At any rate, a great deal of false teaching is due to the assumption that poems known to the critic are of necessity the best.

My lists are a starting-point and a challenge. This challenge has been open for a number of years and no one has yet taken it up. There have been general complaints, but no one has offered a rival list, or put forward particular poems as better examples of a postulated virtu or quality.

Years ago a musician said to me: 'But isn't there a place where you can get it all [meaning all of poetry] as in Bach?'

There isn't. I believe if a man will really learn Greek he can get nearly 'all of it' in Homer.

I have never read half a page of **Homer** without finding melodic invention, I mean melodic invention that I didn't already know. I have, on the other hand, found also in Homer the imaginary spectator, which in 1918 I still thought was Henry James' particular property.

Homer says, 'an experienced soldier would have noticed'. The sheer literary qualities in Homer are such that a physician has written a book to prove that Homer must have been an army doctor. (When he describes certain blows and their effect, the wounds are said to be accurate, and the description fit for coroner's inquest.)

Another French scholar has more or less shown that the geography of the Odyssey is correct geography; not as

43

you would find it if you had a geography book and a map, but as it would be in a 'periplum', that is, as a coasting sailor would find it.

The news in the Odyssey is still news. Odysseus is still 'very human', by no means a stuffed shirt, or a pretty figure taken down from a tapestry. It is very hard to describe some of the homeric conversation, the irony, etc., without neologisms, which my publishers have suggested I eschew. The only readable translation of this part of Homer known to me was made by Amadis Jamyn, secretaire et lecteur ordinaire du Roy (Henry III of France). He refers to Odysseus as 'ce rusé personnage'.

You can't tuck Odysseus away with Virgil's Aeneas. Odysseus is emphatically 'the wise guy', the downy, the hard-boiled Odysseus. His companions have most of them something that must have been the Greek equivalent of shell-shock.

And the language of the conversations is just as alive as when one of Edgar Wallace's characters says, 'We have lost a client'.

W. B. Yeats is sufficiently venerated to be cited now in a school book. The gulf between Homer and Virgil can be illustrated profanely by one of Yeats' favourite anecdotes.

A plain sailor man took a notion to study Latin, and his teacher tried him with Virgil; after many lessons he asked him something about the hero.

Said the sailor: 'What hero?'

Said the teacher: 'What hero, why, Aeneas, the hero.'

Said the sailor: 'Ach, a hero, him a hero? Bigob, I t'ought he waz a priest.'

.   .   .   .

44

There is one quality which unites all great and perdurable writers, you don't NEED schools and colleges to keep 'em alive. Put them out of the curriculum, lay them in the dust of libraries, and once in every so often a chance reader, unsubsidized and unbribed, will dig them up again, put them in the light again, without asking favours.

Virgil was the official literature of the middle ages, but 'everybody' went on reading Ovid. Dante makes all his acknowledgements to Virgil (having appreciated the best of him), but the direct and indirect effect of Ovid on Dante's actual writing is possibly greater than Virgil's.

Virgil came to life again in 1514 partly or possibly because Gavin Douglas knew the sea better than Virgil had.

The lover of Virgil who wishes to bring a libel action against me would be well advised to begin his attack by separating the part of the Aeneid in which Virgil was directly interested (one might almost say, the folk-lore element) from the parts he wrote chiefly because he was trying to write an epic poem.

You have been promised a text-book, and I perhaps ramble on as if we had been taken outdoors to study botany from the trees instead of from engravings in classroom. That is partly the fault of people who complained that I gave them lists without saying why I had chosen such-and-such authors.

YOU WILL NEVER KNOW either why I chose them, or why they were worth choosing, or why you approve or disapprove my choice, until you go to the TEXTS, the originals.

And the quicker you go to the texts the less need there will be for your listening to me or to any other long-winded critic.

A man who has climbed the Matterhorn may prefer Derbyshire to Switzerland, but he won't think the Peak is the highest mountain in Europe.

An epic is a poem including history.

Greek Drama depends greatly on the hearer or reader knowing Homer. It is my firm opinion that there are a great many defects in Greek drama. I should never try to stop a man's reading **Aeschylus** or **Sophocles**. There is nothing in this book that ought in any way to curtail a man's reading or to prevent his reading anything he enjoys.

Ultimately, I suppose, any man with decent literary curiosity will read the *Agamemnon* of Aeschylus, but if he has seriously considered drama as a means of expression he will see that whereas the medium of poetry is WORDS, the medium of drama is people moving about on a stage and using words. That is, the words are only a part of the medium and the gaps between them, or deficiencies in their meaning, can be made up by 'action'.

People who have given the matter dispassionate and careful attention are fairly convinced that the maximum charge of verbal meaning cannot be used on the stage, save for very brief instants. 'It takes time to get it over', etc.

This is not a text-book of the drama, or of dramatic criticism. It is unfair to a dramatist to consider his

46

WORDS, or even his words and versification, as if that were the plenum of his performance.

Taken as READING MATTER, I do NOT believe that the Greek dramatists are up to Homer. Even Aeschylus is rhetorical. Even in the *Agamemnon* there are quantities of words which do not function as reading matter, i.e., are not necessary to our understanding of the subject.

SAPPHO

I HAVE put the great name on the list, because of antiquity and because there is really so little left that one may as well read it as omit it. Having read it, you will be told there is nothing better. I know of no better ode than the POIKILOTHRON. So far as I know, Catullus is the only man who has ever mastered the lady's metre.

For the sake of the student's mental clarity, and for the maintenance of order in his ideas, he will, I think, find it always advantageous to read the oldest poem of a given kind that he can get hold of.

There may be very, very learned Greek specialists who can find something in Alexandrine epigram that isn't already in Sappho and Ibycus, but we are here considering the start of our studies.

For the sake of keeping a proportionate evaluation, it would be well to start by thinking of the different KINDS of expression, the different WAYS of getting meaning into words, rather than of particular things said or particular comments made.

The term 'meaning' cannot be restricted to strictly

47

intellectual or 'coldly intellectual' significance. The how much you mean it, the how you feel about meaning it, can all be 'put into language'.

I took my critical life in my hand, some years ago, when I suggested that Catullus was in some ways a better writer than Sappho, not for melopoeia, but for economy of words. I don't in the least know whether this is true. One should start with an open mind.

The snobbism of the renaissance held that all Greek poetry was better than ANY Latin poetry. The most intelligent of the Quattrocento Latinists, Basinio of Parma, proclaimed a very different thesis; he held that you couldn't write Latin poetry really well unless you knew Greek. That is, you see, very different. In the margins of his Latin narrative you can still see the tags of Homer that he was using to keep his melodic sense active.

I don't believe that any Latin author is in measurable distance of Homer. I doubt if Catullus is inferior to Sappho. I doubt if Propertius is a millimetre inferior to his Greek antecedents; Ovid is for us a store-house of a vast mass of matter that we cannot NOW get from the Greek. He is uneven. He is clear. His verse is as lucid as prose. Metrically he is not a patch on Catullus or Propertius.

Perhaps the student will now begin to see that I am trying to give him a list of authors who are unsurpassed IN THEIR OWN DOMAIN, whereas the writers whom I omit are demonstrably INFERIOR to one or more of the writers I include, and their inferiority can be computed on some particular basis.

· · · · ·

48

HAVE PATIENCE, I am not insisting even now on your learning a multitude of strange languages, I will even tell you, in due course, what you can do if you can read only English.

To put it another way, I am, after all these years, making a list of books that I still re-read; that I keep on my desk and look into now and again.

Chapter Five

1

The great break in European literary history is the change over from inflected to uninflected language. And a great deal of critical nonsense has been written by people who did not realize the difference.

Greek and Latin are inflected, that is, nouns, verbs and adjectives have little tags, or wagging tails, and the tags tell whether the noun is subject or predicate; they indicate that which acts and that which is acted upon, directly or indirectly, or that which is just standing around, in more or less causal relation, etc.

Most of these tags were forgotten as our modern contemporary European languages evolved. German, the least developed, retains most inflection.

The best way of using a language with these signs and labels attached to the words, is NOT the best way to use a language which has to be written in a certain order if it is to be clear.

It makes a difference in English whether you say man sees dog   [or]   dog sees man.

In Latin either canis or canem, homo or hominem, can come first without the sentence being the least bit ambiguous.

When Milton writes

> 'Him who disobeys me disobeys'

he is, quite simply, doing wrong to his mother tongue. He meant

> Who disobeys him, disobeys me.

It is perfectly easy to understand WHY he did it, but his reasons prove that Shakespeare and several dozen other men were better poets. Milton did it because he was chock a block with Latin. He had studied his English not as a living language, but as something subject to theories.

> Who disobeys him, disobeys me,

doesn't make good verse. The sound is better where the idiom is bad. When the writing is masterly one does NOT have to excuse it or to hunt up the reason for perpetrating the flaw.

2

My list of mediaeval poems is perhaps harder to justify.

I once got a man to start translating the **Seafarer** into Chinese. It came out almost directly into Chinese verse, with two solid ideograms in each half-line.

Apart from the Seafarer I know no other European poems of the period that you can hang up with the 'Exile's Letter' of Li Po, displaying the West on a par with the Orient.

There are passages of Anglo-Saxon as good as paragraphs of the Seafarer, but I have not found any whole poem of the same value. The Spanish Cid is clear narrative, and the sagas of Grettir and Burnt Nial prove that narrative capacity didn't die out.

I don't know that a contemporary writer could learn anything about writing from the sagas that he couldn't learn better from Flaubert, but Skarpheddin's jump and slide on the ice, and the meeting of Grettir, or whoever it was, with the bear do not fade from one's memory. You can't believe it is fiction. Some Icelander on a ledge must at some time have saved himself by lopping off the outside paw of a bear, and so making the brute lose its balance. This is in a sense phanopoeia, the throwing of an image on the mind's retina.

The defect of earlier imagist propaganda was not in misstatement but in incomplete statement. The diluters took the handiest and easiest meaning, and thought only of the STATIONARY image. If you can't think of imagism or phanopoeia as including the moving image, you will have to make a really needless division of fixed image and praxis or action.

I have taken to using the term phanopoeia to get away from irrelevant particular connotations tangled with a particular group of young people who were writing in 1912.

3

It is mainly for the sake of the melopoeia that one investigates troubadour poetry.

One might almost say that the whole culture of the age, at any rate the mass of the purely literary culture of the age, from 1050 to 1250 and on till 1300, was concentrated on one aesthetic problem, which, as Dante put it, 'includes the whole art'.

That 'whole art' consisted in putting together about six strophes of poesy so that the words and the tune should be welded together without joint and without wem.

The best smith, as Dante called **Arnaut Daniel**, made the birds sing IN HIS WORDS; I don't mean that he merely referred to birds singing——

In the canzone beginning

> L'aura amara
> Fals bruoills brancutz
> Clarzir
> > Quel doutz espeissa ab fuoills.
> Els letz
> Becs
> Dels auzels ramencz
> Ten balps e mutz
> > > > etc.

And having done it in that one strophe he kept them at it, repeating the tune, and finding five rhymes for each of seventeen rhyme sounds in the same order.

Having done that he constructed another perfect strophe, where the bird call interrupts the verse.

> Cadahus
> En son us

Mas pel us

Estauc clus.

That again for six strophes WITH the words making
sense.

The music of these songs has been lost, but the tradition
comes up again, over three centuries later.

Clement Janequin wrote a chorus, with sounds for the
singers of the different parts of the chorus. These sounds
would have no literary or poetic value if you took the music
away, but when Francesco da Milano reduced it for the
lute, the birds were still in the music. And when Münch
transcribed it for modern instruments the birds were still
there. They ARE still there in the violin part.

That is why the monument outlasts the bronze casting.

Against this craft, I put, with quite definite intention,
the syncopation or the counterpoint of the Syrian Greek
Death of Adonis, with, shall we say, **Bion's** jazz beat
running cross-wise.

As instance of how the life of a work of art is something that just won't stay nailed down in a coffin: The
Kennedy-Frasers found some music in the outer Hebrides
that fits the Beowulf, or at any rate that some of the
Beowulf fits. It is the 'Aillte'. I heard it in concert, and
racked my mind to think where it fitted. It wouldn't go to
the Seafarer. Two lines fitted a bit of the Beowulf, then the
next wouldn't fit. I skipped a line of the Beowulf, and went
on. The Kennedy-Frasers had omitted a line of the music

at that point because it didn't seem to them to have an inherent musical interest.

The point of the foregoing strophes, or at least one dimension of their workmanship, can be grasped by anyone, whether they know Provençal or not.

What is to be said for the quality of **Ventadour** in the best moments, or of **Sordello**, where there is nothing but the perfection of the movement, nothing salient in the thought or the rhyme scheme? You have to have known Provençal a long time perhaps before you perceive the difference between this work and another.

Nevertheless, if you are to know the dimensions of English verse melody a few centuries later, you must find your measures or standards in Provence. The Minnesingers were contemporary; you can contrast the finesse of the south Latin, with the thicker pigment of **Heinrich von Morungen** or **Von der Vogelweide**.

Germans claim that German poetry has developed since the middle ages. My own belief is that Goethe and Stefan George at their lyric best are doing nothing that hadn't already been done better or as well. Burchardt's best verse to-day is in his translations of the Vita Nuova.

During seven centuries a lot of subject matter of no great present interest has been stuffed into German verse that is not very skilful. I can see no reason why a foreign writer should study it.

I see every reason for studying Provençal verse (a little of it, say thirty or fifty poems) from **Guillaume de Poictiers,**

Bertrand de Born and **Sordello**. **Guido** and **Dante** in Italy, **Villon** and **Chaucer** in France and England, had their root in Provence: their art, their artistry, and a good deal of their thought.

European civilization or, to use an abominated word, 'culture' can be perhaps best understood as a mediaeval trunk with wash after wash of classicism going over it. That is not the whole story, but to understand it, you must think of that series of perceptions, as well as of anything that has existed or subsisted unbroken from antiquity.

This book can't be the whole history. Specifically we are considering the development of language as a means of registration.

The Greeks and Romans used one set of devices, one set of techniques. The Provençals developed a different one, not in respect to phanopoeia, but in respect to melopoeia, AFTER a change in the language system (from inflected, to progressively less inflected speech).

The quantitative verse of the ancients was replaced by syllabic verse, as they say in the school books. It would be better to say that the theories applied by grammarians to Latin verse, as the descendant of Greek, were dropped;

And that fitting *motz el son* of words to tune replaced the supposedly regular spondees, dactyls, etc.

The question of the relative duration of syllables has never been neglected by men with susceptible ears.

I particularly want to keep off these technical details. The way to learn the music of verse is to listen to it.

56

After that the student can buy a metronome, or study solfège to perfect his sense of relative duration and of pitch. The present booklet is concerned with language.

For the specific difference between Provence and Italy or the 'progress' from Arnaut Daniel to Sordello, to Cavalcanti and Dante, the reader who cannot and will not read Italian, can, if he like, refer to my descriptive criticism.

Without knowing Dante, Guido Cavalcanti and Villon, no one can judge the attained maxima of certain kinds of writing.

Without the foregoing MINIMUM of poetry in other languages you simply will not know 'where English poetry comes'.

Chapter Six

For *those who read only English*, I have done what I can.

I have translated the TA HIO so that they can learn where to start THINKING. And I have translated the Seafarer; so that they can see more or less where English poetry starts.

I don't know how they can get an idea of Greek. There are no satisfactory English translations.

A Latin crib can do a good deal. If you read French you can get the STORY of the Iliads and of the beginning of the Odyssey from Salel and Jamyn, or rather you could if their books weren't out of print. (I know no edition more recent than 1590.) Chapman is something different. See my notes on the Elizabethan translators.

You can get Ovid, or rather Ovid's stories in Golding's *Metamorphoses*, which is the most beautiful book in the language (my opinion and I suspect it was Shakespeare's).

Marlowe translated the *Amores*.

And before that Gavin Douglas had made something of the Aeneids that I, at any rate, like better than Virgil's Latin.

From Chaucer you can learn (1) whatever came over into the earliest English that one can read without a dictionary, but for which a glossary is needed; (2) and the specifically ENGLISH quality or component. Landor's dialogues of Chaucer, Petrarch and Boccaccio, are the best real criticism of Chaucer we have.

There are anthologies of early English verse. Sidgwick has made the best one I half remember.

After Chaucer, come Gavin Douglas, Golding and Marlowe with their 'translations'.

Then comes Shakespeare in division: the sonnets where he is, I think, practising his craft. The lyrics where he is learning, I believe from Italian song-books in which the WORDS were printed WITH the music.

The plays, especially the series of history plays, which form the true English EPOS,

as distinct from the bastard Epic, the imitation, the constructed counterfeit.

It would be particularly against the grain of the whole ideogrammic method for me to make a series of general statements concerning Elizabethan katachrestical language.

The way to study Shakespeare's language is to study it side by side with something different and of equal extent.

The proper antagonist is Dante, who is of equal size and DIFFERENT. To study Shakespeare's language merely in comparison with the DECADENCE of the same thing doesn't give one's mind any leverage.

There is Shakespearian song. There is the language made to be SPOKEN, perhaps even to be ranted.

Felix Schelling has evolved or quoted the theory that Shakespeare wanted to be a poet, but that when he couldn't make a career of it, he took to writing stage plays, not altogether liking the form.

If the student can't measure Shakespeare against Dante, the next alternative is possibly to measure his language against the prose manifestation of Voltaire, Stendhal, Flaubert, or of Fielding—if you cannot read French.

You can't judge any chemical's action merely by putting it with more of itself. To know it, you have got to know its limits, both what it is and what it is not. What substances are harder or softer, what more resilient, what more compact.

You can't measure it merely by itself diluted with some neutral substance.

．　．　．　．　．

TO BREAK UP THE BOREDOM, I have suggested the great translators . . . for an anthology, shall we say, of the poems that don't put me to sleep.

There are passages of Marlowe. Donne has written the only English poem ('The Ecstasy') that can be set against Cavalcanti's Donna mi Prega. The two are not in the least alike. Their problems are utterly different.

The great lyric age lasted while Campion made his own music, while Lawes set Waller's verses, while verses, if not actually sung or set to music, were at least made with the intention of going to music.

Music rots when it gets *too far* from the dance. Poetry atrophies when it gets too far from music.

There are three kinds of melopoeia, that is, verse made to sing; to chant or intone; and to speak.

The older one gets the more one believes in the first.

One reads prose for the subject matter.

Glance at Burton's 'anatomy' as a curiosity, a sample of NON VERSE which has qualities of poetry but that cannot be confounded with it.

English prose is alive in Florio's Montaigne; Urquhart's Rabelais;

Fielding; Jane Austen; the novelists that everyone reads; Kipling; H. James. James' prefaces tell what 'writing a novel' means.

Chapter Seven

It doesn't matter which leg of your table you make first, so long as the table has four legs and will stand up solidly when you have finished it.

Mediocre poetry is in the long run the same in all countries. The decadence of Petrarchism in Italy and the 'rice powder poetry' in China arrive at about the same level of weakness despite the difference in idiom.

Chapter Eight

Coming round again to the starting-point.

Language is a means of communication. To charge language with meaning to the utmost possible degree, we have, as stated, the three chief means:

I throwing the object (fixed or moving) on to the visual imagination.

II inducing emotional correlations by the sound and rhythm of the speech.

III inducing both of the effects by stimulating the associations (intellectual or emotional) that have remained in the receiver's consciousness in relation to the actual words or word groups employed.

(phanopoeia, melopoeia, logopoeia)

Incompetence will show in the use of too many words. The reader's first and simplest test of an author will be to look for words that do not function; that contribute nothing to the meaning OR that distract from the MOST important factor of the meaning to factors of minor importance.

·   ·   ·   ·   ·

One definition of beauty is: aptness to purpose.

Whether it is a good definition or not, you can readily see that a good deal of BAD criticism has been written by men who assume that an author is trying to do what he is NOT trying to do.

Incredible as it now seems, the bad critics of Keats' time found his writing 'obscure', which meant that they couldn't understand WHY Keats wrote.

Most human perceptions date from a long time ago, or are derivable from perceptions that gifted men have had long before we were born. The race discovers, and rediscovers.

TESTS AND COMPOSITION EXERCISES

I

1 Let the pupils exchange composition papers and see how many and what useless words have been used—how many words that convey nothing new.

2 How many words that obscure the meaning.

3 How many words out of their usual place, and whether this alteration makes the statement in any way more interesting or more energetic.

4 Whether a sentence is ambiguous; whether it really means more than one thing or more than the writer in-

tended; whether it can be so read as to mean something different.

5 Whether there is something clear on paper, but ambiguous if spoken aloud.

II

It is said that Flaubert taught De Maupassant to write. When De Maupassant returned from a walk Flaubert would ask him to describe someone, say a concierge whom they would both pass in their next walk, and to describe the person so that Flaubert would recognize, say, the concierge and not mistake her for some other concierge and not the one De Maupassant had described.

SECOND SET

1 Let the pupil write the description of a tree.

2 Of a tree without mentioning the name of the tree (larch, pine, etc.) so that the reader will not mistake it for the description of some other kind of tree.

3 Try some object in the class-room.

4 Describe the light and shadow on the school-room clock or some other object.

5 If it can be done without breach of the peace, the pupil could write descriptions of some other pupil. The author suggests that the pupil should not describe the instructor, otherwise the description might become a vehicle of emotion, and subject to more complicated rules of composition than the class is yet ready to cope with.

In all these descriptions the test would be accuracy and vividness, the pupil receiving the other's paper would be the gauge. He would recognize or not recognize the object or person described.

Rodolfo Agricola in an edition dating from fifteen hundred and something says one writes: *ut doceat, ut moveat ut delectet*, to teach, to move or to delight.

.   .   .   .   .

66

A great deal of bad criticism is due to men not seeing which of these three motives underlies a given composition.

The converse processes, not considered by the pious teachers of antiquity, would be to obscure, to bamboozle or mislead, and to bore.

The reader or auditor is at liberty to remain passive and submit to these operations if he so choose.

FURTHER TESTS

LET the pupil examine a given piece of writing, say, the day's editorial in a newspaper, to see whether the writer is trying to conceal something; to see whether he is 'veiling his meaning'; whether he is afraid to say what he thinks; whether he is trying to appear to think without really doing any thinking.

Metrical writing

1   Let the pupil try to write in the metre of any poem he likes.

2   Let him write words to a well-known tune.

3   Let him try to write words to the same tune in such a way that the words will not be distorted when one sings them.

4   Let the pupil write a poem in some strophe form he likes.

5   Let him parody some poem he finds ridiculous, either because of falsity in the statement, or falsity in the disposition of the writer, or for pretentiousness, of one kind or another, or for any other reason that strikes his risible faculties, his sense of irony.

The gauging pupil should be asked to recognize what author is parodied. And whether the joke is on the parodied or the parodist. Whether the parody exposes a real defect, or merely makes use of an author's mechanism to expose a more trivial contents.

Note: No harm has ever yet been done a good poem by this process. FitzGerald's *Rubaiyat* has survived hundreds of parodies, that are not really parodies either of Omar or FitzGerald, but only poems written in that form of strophe.

Note: There is a tradition that in Provence it was considered plagiarism to take a man's form, just as it is now considered plagiarism to take his subject matter or plot.

Poems frankly written to another man's strophe form or tune were called 'Sirventes', and were usually satirical.

FURTHER TESTS

1 Let the pupils in exchanging themes judge whether the theme before them really says anything.

2 Let them judge whether it tells them anything or 'makes them see anything' they hadn't noticed before, especially in regard to some familiar scene or object.

3 Variant: whether the writer really had to KNOW something about the subject or scene before being able to write the page under consideration.

The question of a word or phrase being 'useless' is not merely a numerical problem.

Anatole France in criticizing French dramatists pointed out that **on the stage**, the words must give time for the action; they must give time for the audience to take count of what is going on.

Even on the printed page there is an analogous ease.

Tacitus in writing Latin can use certain forms of condensation that don't necessarily translate advantageously into English.

The reader will often misjudge a condensed writer by trying to read him too fast.

The secret of popular writing is never to put more on a given page than the common reader can lap off it with no strain WHATSOEVER on his habitually slack attention.

Anatole France is said to have spent a great deal of time searching for the *least possible* variant that would turn the most worn-out and commonest phrases of journalism into something distinguished.

Such research is sometimes termed 'classicism'.

This is the greatest possible remove from the usual English stylist's trend or urge toward a style different from everyone else's.

BASIS

THERE is no use, or almost none, in my publisher's asking me to make English Literature as prominent as possible. I mean, not if I am to play fair with the student. You cannot learn to write by reading English.

If you are affected by early poets you produce 'costume of the period'. Chaucer is incomprehensible without a glossary. Elizabethanisms are easily recognizable as ancient finery.

Chaucer did not MAKE his art. This doesn't detract from his glory as a great and very human writer. He took over his art from the French. He wrote about the astrolabe. Dante wrote *On the Common Tongue*, a treatise on language and versification.

The language of the Elizabethans is upholstered. The age of Shakespeare was the GREAT AGE par excellence, it was the age when the language was not cut and dried, when the auditor liked the WORDS; he got, probably, as much kick out of 'multitudinous seas incarnadine', as the readers of the Yellow Book got out of a twisted epigram.

This wasn't a class interest; in Spain at that time the most effective critic of plays was a cobbler. But the language was a made-up artificial speech; it was the age of Euphues in England and of Gongora in Spain.

How did it get that way?

The cult of Latin. After the thinness, the 'transparency', of mediaeval authors, the reading world was once again

71

drunk on antiquity, Greece and Rome; the most educated wrote in Latin; each writer wanted to show that he knew more Latin than the other; there are bales of their Latin poems; the Italians took over the style and extended the vocabularly, the Spaniards and English imitated the Italians; Camoens tried it in Portugal. It was the gold rush for the largest vocabulary. I suspect that Marlowe started to parody himself in Hero and Leander. He had begun with serious intentions.

I recognize that this suspicion may be an error.

The next phase in France and England was to attempt to squeeze the katachrestical rhetoric into a strait-waist-coat.

This doesn't mean that the reader can afford to be ignorant of the best work of either period. He can look for real speech in Shakespeare and find it in plenty IF he knows what to look for.

The so-called prose of several centuries is concerned with—or at least your teachers will recommend it for—'sentence structure'.

If you can read only English, start on Fielding. There you have a solid foundation. His language is neither strait-laced nor all trimmings.

After which I suppose one should recommend Miss Jane Austen. And that makes almost the list, i.e.:

The list of things safe to read an hour before you start

writing, as distinct from the books a non-writing reader can peruse for enjoyment.

But aren't there well-written books and poems in English? There indubitably are.

But can anyone estimate Donne's best poems save in relation to Cavalcanti?

I do not believe it.

There was a period when the English lyric quality, the juncture of note and melody was very high. But to gauge that height, a knowledge of Provence is extremely useful.

If you want to write satiric couplets, or 'iambic couplets', you indubitably can learn a good deal from Pope and Crabbe.

Wordsworth got rid of a lot of trimmings, but there are vast stretches of deadness in his writing. Artists are the antennae of the race. Wordsworth vibrates to a very limited range of stimuli, and he was not conscious of the full problem of writing.

The problem of sentence structure was undeniably discussed during several centuries.

'A carpenter can put boards together, but a good carpenter would know seasoned wood from green.'

The mere questions of constructing and assembling clauses, of parsing and grammar are not enough. Such study ended in a game of oratory, now parodied in detective stories when they give the learned counsel's summing-up.

The development after these structural exercises occurred chiefly in France: Stendhal, Flaubert.

An attempt to set down things as they are, to find the word that corresponds to the thing, the statement that portrays, and presents, instead of making a comment, however brilliant, or an epigram.

Flaubert is the archetype. The Brothers Goncourt codified and theorized and preached Flaubert's practice. Flaubert never stopped experimenting. Before he had finished he called his *Salammbo* 'cette vieille toquade', or old charade in fancy clothes. Laforgue parodied this phrase of Flaubert, in a sublime divertissement, a play, in the best sense, of words and of images.

Maupassant put the system into high gear, accelerated it, lightened it, and all subsequent short-story writers, Kipling, etc., have learned from Maupassant.

If a reader wants the dilutation, if he is content NOT to go to the fountain-head, he can indubitably find a fair competence in short-story writing in current publications. E.g. the current *Criterion* publishes a story showing what seem to be traces of Hemingway, and one doesn't even know they are Hemingway at first hand.

THE FIRST PHASE of anyone's writing always shows them doing something 'like' something they have heard or read.

The majority of writers never pass that stage.

In London as late as 1914 the majority of poetasters still resented the idea that poetry was an art, they thought you ought to do it without any analysis, it was still expected to 'pour forth'.

The usual game of quibbling over half truth, starts just here. The best work probably does pour forth, but it does so AFTER the use of the medium has become 'second nature', the writer need no more think about EVERY DETAIL, than Tilden needs to think about the position of every muscle in every stroke of his tennis. The force, the draw, etc., follow the main intention, without damage to the unity of the act.

The student having studied geometry and physics or chemistry knows that in one you begin with simple forms, in another with simple substances.

The analogous method in literature is to take the author, poem or tale where a given quality exists in its purest form or its highest degree.

The key invention, the first case or first available illustration.

Contemporary book-keeping uses a 'loose-leaf' system to keep the active part of a business separate from its archives. That doesn't mean that accounts of new customers are kept apart from accounts of old customers, but that the business still in being is not loaded up with accounts of business that no longer functions.

You can't cut off books written in 1934 from those written in 1920 or 1932 or 1832, at least you can't derive much advantage from a *merely* chronological category, though chronological relation may be important. If not that post hoc means propter hoc, at any rate the composition of books written in 1830 can't be due to those written in 1933, though the value of old work is constantly affected by the value of the new.

This is true not only of single works but of whole categories. Max Ernst's designs send a great deal of psychological novel writing into the discard. The cinema supersedes a great deal of second-rate narrative, and a great deal of theatre.

A film form may perfectly well be a better form (intellectually) than a stage form.

A film may make better use of 60 per cent of all narrative dramatic material. Each case can be decided on its own merits.

In all cases one test will be, 'could this material have been made more efficient in some other medium?'

This statement is simply an extension of the 1914 Vorticist manifesto.

A distinguished novelist complained that no directions for major form were given in *How to Read*.

In apology: It is a waste of time to listen to people talking of things they have not understood sufficiently to perform.

You can study *part* of the art of novel construction in the novels of Trollope.

You can learn something of a great writer's attitude toward the art of the novel in the prefaces of Henry James' collected edition.

Had I written a dozen good novels I might presume to add something.

The Goncourts' preface to Germinie Lacerteux gives the most succinct statement of the views of the nineteenth-century realists. It is the declaration of the rights of men trying to record 'L'histoire morale contemporaine', the history of contemporary moral disposition, the history of the estimation of values in contemporary behaviour.

In an introductory work like the present, you are not being asked to decide what theories are correct, but to what degree different writers have been efficient in expressing their thought.

LIBERTY

ONE liberty of the text-book (as a form of writing) is that it permits refrain, repetition.

But, teacher, mustn't we read . . . Wordsworth?

Yes, my children, you can and may read anything you like. But instead of having me or anyone else tell you what is on the page, you should look for yourselves.

Does Mr. Wordsworth sometimes use words that express nothing in particular?

Mr. Swinburne is famed or infamed for having used a great many which express nothing but 'colour' or 'splendour'. It has been said that he used the same adjectives to describe a woman and a sunset.

EXERCISE

IT would be a very good exercise to take parallel passages of these two poets, the first so very famous, and the second one so very much decried at the present time, and see how many useless words each uses, how many which contribute nothing, how many which contribute nothing very definite.

A similar exercise could be performed on Swinburne and Milton.

XIXth Century

COMING nearer our own times, the student who can read French is invited to verify my suspicion that the technique in Gautier's early work *Albertus* is about as good as that of the best English verse in the 1890's. The English of that period added little to the sum of knowledge in poetic practice.

To understand what was invented after 1830 I recommend:

Théophile Gautier *Emaux et Camées*, Corbière, Rimbaud, Laforgue.

To see how a man could write a single line or a brief paragraph of verse.

In England Robert Browning refreshed the form of monologue or dramatic monologue or 'Persona', the ancestry of which goes back at least to Ovid's Heroides which are imaginary letters in verse, and to Theocritus, and is thence lost in antiquity.

STUDY

FRENCH very brief narrative poems of this period, in the authors listed.

Gautier, Corbière, Rimbaud, Laforgue.

Characters presented: Browning.
How much of Walt Whitman is well written?

If you were compiling an anthology of English what better poets could you find than:
Chaucer.
Gavin Douglas 12 Bukes of Aeneidos.
Golding's *Metamorphoses* translated from Ovid.
Marlowe (*Amores*), passages of his plays.
Shakespeare (Histories, and the lyrics as technical masterwork).
Donne: The Ecstasy.

Song writers: Herrick, Campion, Waller, Dorset, Rochester.

Writers in narrative couplet: Pope, Crabbe.

Pick out the dozen best old ballads.
Pick out the twenty-five best lyrics written between 1500 and 1700 from any of the available anthologies.

Try to find a poem of Byron or Poe without seven serious defects.

Try to find out why the Fitzgerald *Rubaiyat* has gone

into so many editions after having lain unnoticed until Rossetti found a pile of remaindered copies on a second-hand bookstall.

Did the '90's' add anything to English poetry, or did they merely prune Swinburne? and borrow a little from the French symbolistes?

What was there to the Celtic movement?
Apart from, let us say, the influence of Irish ballad rhythm on Yeats' metric?

In no case should the student from now on be TOLD that such and such things are facts about a given body of poetry or about a given poem.
The questions in this exercise do not demand the same answer from any two pupils. They are not asked in order to drag out plain yes and no answers.

Why isn't Walter Savage Landor more read?
Did he write poetry as well as Robert Browning?
How much of his poetry is good?
Has England ever produced an all-round man of letters of equal stature?

If you are trying to find a summary of the conscience of a given century, where would you go to find it?

In early periods you might well seek it in the poetry.
For the centuries after the renaissance you might perhaps have to find it in the prose?

If so, that would mean that prose of those times was in some way more efficient than the poetry?

You have, probably all of you, your favourite writers.
What would happen to you if you started writing immediately after you had been reading

A,

B,

or C?

Do they use a dialect? and would you 'catch it'?

If you wanted to say something they hadn't said, or something of a different kind, would their manner of writing make your statement more accurate?

more interesting?

. . . . .

Do you know why you like . . . . . A

B

C

(pupil can fill the blanks in at his own discretion).

Do you in any way distinguish between writers whom you 'like' and those whom you 'respect'?

Why, and how?

PERCEPTION

'ARTISTS are the antennae of the race.'

Can you be interested in the writings of men whose general perceptions are below the average?

. . . .

I am afraid that even here the answer is not a straight 'No'.

There is a much more delicate question:

Can you be interested in the work of a man who is blind to 80 per cent of the spectrum? to 30 per cent of the spectrum?

Here the answer is, curiously enough, yes IF . . . if his perceptions are hypernormal in any part of the spectrum he can be of very great use as a writer——

though perhaps not of very great 'weight'. This is where the so-called crack-brained genius comes in. The concept of genius as akin to madness has been carefully fostered by the inferiority complex of the public.

A graver issue needs biological analogy: artists are the antennae; an animal that neglects the warnings of its perceptions needs very great powers of resistance if it is to survive.

Your finer senses are protected, the eye by bone socket, etc.

A nation which neglects the perceptions of its artists declines. After a while it ceases to act, and merely survives.

There is probably no use in telling this to people who can't see it without being told.

Artists and poets undoubtedly get excited and 'overexcited' about things long before the general public.

Before deciding whether a man is a fool or a good artist, it would be well to ask, not only: 'is he excited unduly', but: 'does he see something we don't?'

Is his curious behaviour due to his feeling an oncoming earthquake, or smelling a forest fire which we do not yet feel or smell?

Barometers, wind-gauges, cannot be used as engines.

THE INSTRUCTOR

I The teacher or lecturer is a danger. He very seldom recognizes his nature or his position. The lecturer is a man who must talk for an hour.

France may possibly have acquired the intellectual leadership of Europe when their academic period was cut down to forty minutes.

I also have lectured. The lecturer's first problem is to have enough words to fill forty or sixty minutes. The professor is paid for his time, his results are almost impossible to estimate.

The man who really knows can tell all that is transmissible in a very few words. The economic problem of the teacher (of violin or of language or of anything else) is how to string it out so as to be paid for more lessons.

Be as honest as you like, but the danger is there even when one knows it. I have felt the chill even in this brief booklet. In pure good will, but because one must make a rough estimate, the publishers sent me a contract: 40,000 to 50,000 words. I may run over it, but it introduces a 'factor', a component of error, a distraction from the true problem:

What is the simplest possible statement?

. . . . .

II No teacher has ever failed from ignorance.

That is empiric professional knowledge.

Teachers fail because they cannot 'handle the class'.

Real education must ultimately be limited to men who INSIST on knowing, the rest is mere sheep-herding.

. . . . .

III You can **prove** nothing by analogy. The analogy is either range-finding or fumble. Written down as a lurch toward proof, or at worst elaborated in that aim, it leads mainly to useless argument, BUT a man whose wit teems with analogies will often 'twig' that something is wrong long before he knows why.

Aristotle had something of this sort in mind when he wrote 'apt use of metaphor indicating a swift perception of relations'.

A dozen rough analogies may flash before the quick mind, as so many rough tests which eliminate grossly unfit matter or structure.

It is only after long experience that most men are able to define a thing in terms of its own genus, painting as painting, writing as writing. You can spot the bad critic when he starts by discussing the poet and not the poem.

. . . . .

I mistrust the man who starts with forty-nine variants before stating three or four principles. He may be a very serious character, he may be on his way to a fourth or fifth principle that will in the long run be useful or revolutionary, but I suspect that he is still in the middle of his problem, and not ready to offer an answer.

The inexperienced teacher, fearing his own ignorance, is afraid to admit it. Perhaps that courage only comes when one knows to what extent ignorance is almost universal. Attempts to camouflage it are simply a waste, in the long run, of time.

If the teacher is slow of wit, he may well be terrified by students whose minds move more quickly than his own, but he would be better advised to use the lively pupil for scout work, to exploit the quicker eye or subtler ear as look-out or listening post.

The best musician I know admitted that his sense of precise audition was *intermittent*. But he put it in the form '*moi aussi*', after I had made my own confession.

When you get to the serious consideration of any work of art, our faculties or memories or perceptions are all too 'spotty' to permit anything save mutual curiosity.

There is no man who knows so much about, let us say, a passage between lines 100 to 200 of the sixth book of the Odyssey that he can't learn something by re-reading it WITH his students, not merely TO his students. If he knows Guido's Donna Mi Prega as well as I now know it, meaning microscopically, he can still get a new light by some cross-reference, by some relation between the thing he has examined and re-examined, and some other fine work, similar or dissimilar.

I believe the ideal teacher would approach any master-piece that he was presenting to his class *almost* as if he had never seen it before.

TASTES

THERE is no reason why the same man should like the same books at eighteen and at forty-eight.

There are certain divisions and dissociations that I refrain from making because I do not think that, at my age, I should try to force the taste of a middle-aged man on the younger reader.

Thank heaven there are books that one enjoys MOST before one is twenty-five, and that there are *other* books that one can STILL read at forty-five and still hope to be able to read in the sere and yellow.

Realism, romanticism, men as they are seen, men as they are imagined or 'dramatized', men as they are quite simply known NOT to be. . . .

Consider the anecdote of Jack Dempsey. When Tunney was being touted as the educated boxer, a reporter approached Mr. Dempsey on the subject of literature. I think he mentioned Cashel Byron or some novel in which the ring appears. Dempsey wouldn't have it: 'Agh, it tain't LIKE that.'

The reporter observed that Dempsey had a lurid novel about a Russian Grand Duke. He suggested that if Dempsey had been a Grand Duke he might have found similar discrepancies in the portrayal of old Russian high life.

Dempsey: 'I never *wuz* a Grand Duke.'

Perfectly sincere people say 'you can't teach literature', and what they MEAN by that statement is probably true. You *can* quite distinctly teach a man to distinguish between one kind of a book and another.

Certain verbal manifestations *can* be employed as measures, T squares, voltmeters, or can be used 'for comparison', and familiarity with them can indubitably enable a man to estimate writing in general, and the relative forces, energies and perfections or imperfections of books.

You don't furnish a house entirely with yard sticks and weighing machines.

The authors and books I recommend in this introduction to the study of letters are to be considered AS measuring-rods and voltmeters.

The books listed are books to have in mind, BEFORE you try to measure and evaluate other books. They are, most emphatically, NOT all the books worth reading.

A great deal that you read, you simply need not 'bother about'.

On the other hand, you needn't fall into the silly snobbism that has ruined whole shoals of fancy writers, polite essayists, refined young gents, members of literary cénacles und so weiter.

DISSOCIATE

> 'Man should be prouder of having invented
> the hammer and nail than of having created
> masterpieces of imitation.'   Hegel, quoted
> by Fernand Leger.

> 'The intellectual love of a thing consists
> in understanding its perfections.'
> Spinoza

A GREAT deal of critical rancour has been wasted through
a failure to distinguish between two totally different kinds
of writing.

A Books a man reads to develop his capacities: in order
to know more and perceive more, and more quickly,
than he did before he read them.

and

B Books that are intended and that serve as REPOSE,
dope, opiates, mental beds.

You don't sleep on a hammer or lawn-mower, you don't
drive nails with a mattress. Why should people go on
applying the SAME critical standards to writings as
different in purpose and effect as a lawn-mower and a sofa
cushion?

.   .   .   .   .

There is one technique for the mattress-maker and one for the builder of linotype machines. A technique of construction applies both to bedsteads and automobiles.

The dirtiest book in our language is a quite astute manual telling people how to earn money by writing. The fact that it advocates the maximum possible intellectual degradation should not blind one to its constructive merits.

Certain parts of the technique of narrative writing ARE common to Homer, Rudyard Kipling *and* to Mr. Kipling's star disciple, the late Edgar Wallace.

The only intelligent adverse criticism of my *How to Read* was not an attack on what was in it, but on what I had not been able to put there.

One can't get everything into forty-five pages. But even if I had had 450 at my disposal I should not have attempted a treatise on major form in the novel. I have not written a good novel. I have not written a novel. I don't expect to write any novels and shall not tell anyone else how to do it until I have.

If you want to study the novel, go, READ the best you can find. All that I know about it, I have learned by reading:

Tom Jones, by Fielding.

Tristram Shandy and *The Sentimental Journey* by Sterne (and I don't recommend anyone ELSE to try to do another *Tristram Shandy*).

The novels of Jane Austen and Trollope.

.   .   .   .   .

89

[Note: If you compare the realism of Trollope's novels with the realism of Robert McAlmon's stories you will get a fair idea of what a good novelist means by 'construction'. Trollope depicts a scene or a person, and you can clearly see how he 'leads up to an effect'.]

Continuing:

The novels of Henry James, AND especially the prefaces to his collected edition; which are the one extant great treatise on novel writing in English.

In French you can form a fairly good ideogram from:

Benjamin Constant's *Adolphe*.

The first half of Stendhal's *Rouge et Noir* and the first eighty pages of *La Chartreuse de Parme*.

Madame Bovary, *L'Éducation Sentimentale*, *Trois Contes*, and the unfinished *Bouvard et Pécuchet* of FLAUBERT, with Goncourt's preface to *Germinie Lacerteux*.

After that you would do well to look at Madox Ford's *A Call*.

When you have read James' prefaces and twenty of his other novels, you would do well to read *The Sacred Fount*.

There for perhaps the first time since about 1300 a writer has been able to deal with a sort of content wherewith Cavalcanti had been 'concerned'.

You can get a very brilliant cross-light via Donne. I mean the differences and nuances between psychology in Guido, abstract philosophic statement in Guido, the blend in Donne, and again psychology in Henry James, and in all of them the underlying concept of FORM, the structure of the whole work, including its parts.

.   .   .   .   .

This is a long way from an A B C. In fact it opens the vista of post-graduate study.

. . . . .

N.B.

Jealousy of vigorous-living men has perhaps led in all times to a deformation of criticism and a distorted glorification of the past. Motive does not concern us, but error does. Glorifiers of the past commonly err in their computations because they measure the work of a present DECADE against the best work of a past century or even of a whole group of centuries.

Obviously one man or six men can't produce as many metrical triumphs in five years or in twenty, as five hundred troubadours, with no cinema, no novels, no radio to distract 'em, produced between 1050 and 1300. And the same applies in all departments.

The honest critic must be content to find a VERY LITTLE contemporary work worth serious attention; but he must also be ready to RECOGNIZE that little, and to demote work of the past when a new work surpasses it.

DICHTEN = CONDENSARE[1]

THIS chapter heading is Mr. Bunting's discovery and his prime contribution to contemporary criticism, but the idea is far from new. It is as we have said *ingrained* in the very language of Germany, and it has magnificently FUNC-TIONED, brilliantly functioned.

Pisistratus found the Homeric texts in disorder, we don't quite know what he did about it. The Bible is a compendium, people trimmed it to make it solid. It has gone on for ages, because it wasn't allowed to overrun all the available parchment; a Japanese emperor whose name I have forgotten and whose name you needn't remember, found that there were TOO MANY NOH PLAYS, he picked out 450 and the Noh stage LASTED from 1400 or whenever right down till the day the American navy intruded, and that didn't stop it. Umewaka Minoru started again as soon as the revolution wore off. Ovid's Meta-morphoses are a compendium, not an epic like Homer's; Chaucer's Canterbury Tales are a compendium of all the good yarns Chaucer knew. The Tales have lasted through centuries while the long-winded mediaeval narratives went into museums.

[1] A Japanese student in America, on being asked the difference between prose and poetry, said: Poetry consists of gists and piths.

92

SECTION TWO

EXHIBITS

THE ideal way to present the next section of this booklet
would be to give the quotations WITHOUT any comment
whatever. I am afraid that would be too revolutionary. By
long and wearing experience I have learned that in the
present imperfect state of the world, one MUST tell the
reader. I made a very bad mistake in my INSTIGATIONS,
the book had a plan, I thought the reader would see it.

In the present case I shall not tell the student everything.
The most intelligent students, those who most want to
LEARN, will however encompass that end, and endear
themselves to the struggling author if they will read the
EXHIBITS, and not look at my footnotes until they have
at least tried to find out WHAT THE EXHIBIT IS, and to
guess why I have printed it. For any reader of sufficient
intelligence this should be as good a game as Torquemada's
cross-word abominations. I don't expect it to become ever
as popular, but in an ideal REPUBLIC it would.

Era gia l'ore che volge il disio
Ai naviganti.

Purgatorio VIII, I.

Perch' io non spero di tornar già mai
Ballatetta in Toscana.

Cavalcanti.

S'ils n'ayment fors que pour l'argent
On ne les ayme que pour l'heure.

Villon.

The fire that stirs about her, when she stirs.

Yeats.

Ne maeg werigmod wyrde widhstondan
ne se hreo hyge helpe gefremman
for dhon domgeorne dreorigne oft
in hyra breostcofan bindath faeste.

The Wanderer.

Example of ideogrammic method used by E. P. in *The Serious Artist* in 1913 before having access to the Fenollosa papers.

I was trying to indicate a difference between prose simplicity of statement, and an equal limpidity in poetry, where the perfectly simple verbal order is CHARGED with a much higher potential, an emotional potential.

In that essay I also cited Stendhal's: Poetry with its obligatory comparisons, the mythology the poet don't believe in, his so-called dignity of style, *à la Louis XIV*, and all that trail of what they call poetic ornament, is vastly inferior to prose if you are trying to give a clear and exact idea of the '*mouvements du cœur*'; if you are trying to show what a man feels, you can only do it by clarity.

That was the great turning. The great separation of the roads. After Stendhal saw that, and said it, the poetic bunk of the preceding centuries gave way to the new prose, the creation of Stendhal and Flaubert. Poetry then remained the inferior art until it caught up with the prose of these two writers, which it ultimately did quite largely on the basis of DICHTEN = CONDENSARE.

That did NOT mean it was something more wafty and imbecile than prose, but something charged to a higher potential.

But Chaucer though he kan but lewedly[1]
On metres, and on ryming craftily
Hath seyd hem, in swich Englissh as he kan
Of olde tyme, as knoweth many a man
And if he have noght seyd him, leve[2] brother,
In o[3] book, he hath seyd him in another
For he hath toold of loveris up and doun
Mo[4] than Ovide made of mencioun
In his Epistelles. . . .
In youthe he made[5] of Ceys and Alcione

---

[1] unlearnedly [2] dear [3] o = one [4] Mo = more [5] wrote, made poetry

Chaucer's self-criticism placed in the mouth of the Man
of Lawe. He professes himself untaught in metre, meaning
probably quantitative verse. Skilled in rhyme. The maker
of a compendium comparable to Ovid. He follows a
mediaeval custom and goes on to give a catalogue of his
tales. Dido, Ariadne, Hero and Leander, Laodamia, etc.

Sloth is the root of much bad opinion. It is at times difficult for the author to retain his speech within decorous bounds.

I once heard a man, who has some standing as writer and whom Mr. Yeats was wont to defend, assert that Chaucer's language wasn't English, and that one ought not to use it as basis of discussion, ETC. Such was the depth of London in 1910.

Anyone who is too lazy to master the comparatively small glossary necessary to understand Chaucer deserves to be shut out from the reading of good books for ever.

As to the relative merits of Chaucer and Shakespeare, English opinion has been bamboozled for centuries by a love of the stage, the glamour of the theatre, the love of bombastic rhetoric and of sentimentalizing over actors and actresses; these, plus the national laziness and unwillingness to make the least effort, have completely obscured the values.

People even read translations of Chaucer into a curious compost, which is not modern language but which uses a vocabulary comprehended of sapheads.

Wat se thè kennath

Chaucer had a deeper knowledge of life than Shakespeare.

Let the reader contradict that after reading both authors, if he then chooses to do so.

He had a wider knowledge of life, probably, he had at any rate a better chance.

We can leave the question of the relative chances to their biographers. Let us look at the evidence.

Chaucer wrote when reading was no disgrace. He had forty books, gathered probably at considerable trouble and expense. Shakespeare had at least six good ones. Chaucer cites his sources. There was no contemporary snobbism to inhibit this.

BUT Shakespeare OWES quite as much to his reading as Chaucer does.

Men do not understand BOOKS until they have had a certain amount of life. Or at any rate no man understands a deep book, until he has seen and lived at least part of its contents. The prejudice against books has grown from observing the stupidity of men who have *merely* read books.

Chaucer, beyond this, was a man with whom we could have discussed Fabre and Fraser; he had thought considerably about many things which Shakespeare has not very deeply considered.

Chaucer really does comprehend the thought as well as the life of his time.

The Wife of Bath's theology is not a mere smear. Her attention to the meaning of terms is greater than we find in Lorenzo Medici's imaginary dialogue with Ficino about platonism. This is, in Chaucer, the remains of the middle ages, when men took some care of their terminology.

When she says:

conseilling is nat comandement.

she has a meaning in each of her terms.

Chaucer wrote while England was still a part of Europe, There was one culture from Ferrara to Paris and it extended to England. Chaucer was the greatest poet of his day. He was more compendious than Dante.

He participated in the same culture with Froissart and Boccaccio, the great humane culture that went into Rimini, that spoke Franco-Veneto, that is in the roundels of Froissart and in the doggerel of the Malatesta.

In Shakespeare's time England is already narrowing. Shakespeare as supreme lyric technician is indebted to the Italian song-books, but they are already an EXOTIC.

Chaucer uses French art, the art of Provence, the verse art come from the troubadours. In his world there had lived both Guillaume de Poictiers and Scotus Erigena. But Chaucer was not a foreigner. It was HIS civilization.

He made fun of the hrimm hramm ruff, the decadence of Anglo-Saxon alliteration, the verse written by those who had forgotten the WHY of the Anglo-Saxon bardic narration, and been too insular to learn French. True, Chaucer's name *is* French and not English, his mind is the mind of Europe, not the mind of an annex or an outlying province.

He is Le Grand Translateur. He had found a new language, he had it largely to himself, with the grand opportunity. Nothing spoiled, nothing worn out.

Dante had had a similar opportunity, and taken it, with a look over his shoulder and a few Latin experiments. Chaucer felt his chance. The gulf between Chaucer and Gower can be measured by Gower's hesitation, by his proved unwillingness to 'take a chance'. He had a go at metrical exercises in all three of the current tongues:

English, French and Latin. Books, used in the wrong way. The hunt for a subject, etc.

He was the perfect type of English secondary writer, condemned recently but for all time by Henri Davray with his:

'Ils cherchent des sentiments pour les accommoder à leur vocabulaire'.

They hunt for sentiments to fit into their vocabulary.

Chaucer and Shakespeare have both an insuperable courage in tackling any, but absolutely any, thing that arouses their interest.

No one will ever gauge or measure English poetry until they know how much of it, how full a gamut of its qualities, is already THERE ON THE PAGE of Chaucer.

Logopoeia, phanopoeia, melopoeia; the English technique of lyric and of narrative, and the full rich flow of his human contact.

This last term has been degraded and demoted or narrowed down until it excludes all the more complicated, the less usual activities of human feeling and understanding. It is used almost as if it could refer only to low life.

. . . . .

Chaucer is aware of life . . . parity with Shakespeare. He is informed, and understands the intellectual conquests of Europe . . . in a way that Will Shakespeare probably did not. . . . . .

He is open minded, let us say to folk-lore, to the problems Frazer broaches, in a way that Shakespeare certainly was not.

Shakespeare was greatly indifferent. He was fanciful. He was a technical master. The gross and utter stupidity and obtuseness of Milton was never more apparent than in his supercilious reference to 'Woodnotes wild'.

The best thing I ever heard in Dr. Schelling's class-room was the theory that Shakespeare wanted to be a poet but that he had to take to the writing of plays.

He is, probably, if terms of magnitude mean anything, 'the world's greatest dramatist'. Along with Ibsen and Aeschylus.

But it would be very rash to say that he is a better poet than Chaucer, or that he knew more (or ? as much) about life.

Chaucer's culture was wider than Dante's, Petrarch is immeasurably inferior to both. You would not be far out if you chose to consider Chaucer as the father of 'litterae humaniores' for Europe.

Not that the continent found it out. But for *our* purposes we can perfectly well base the whole of our study of the renaissance on Master Geoffrey, the savant who knew as much of the hostler as did the deer-snatcher of Stratford, who knew probably a great deal more of the merchant, certainly more of diplomacy and the ways of the world of power. Which doesn't mean that he has left a better record, or anticipated the revolt of later time.

103

IF Chaucer represents the great mellowing and the dawn of a new paideuma, Villon, the first voice of man broken by bad economics, represents also the end of a tradition, the end of the mediaeval dream, the end of a whole body of knowledge, fine, subtle, that had run from Arnaut to Guido Cavalcanti, that had lain in the secret mind of Europe for centuries, and which is far too complicated to deal with in a primer of reading.

The hardest, the most authentic, the most absolute poet of France. The under dog, the realist, also a scholar. But with the mediaeval dream hammered out of him.

An insuperable technician. Whose art also came from Provence.

I have scamped this paragraph. I have used mediaeval dream to avoid writing a folio in 900 pages.

I don't use the term to mean merely fanciful ornamentation with daisies and dickey birds; I don't mean an escape mechanism. I mean a very complicated structure of knowledge and perception, the paradise of the human mind under enlightenment. All of which, I repeat, cannot be dealt with in a 'first book on reading'.

Technically speaking, translation of Villon is extremely difficult because he rhymes on the exact word, on a word meaning sausages, for example.

The grand bogies for young men who want really to learn strophe writing are Catullus and Villon. I personally have been reduced to setting them to music as I cannot translate them. Swinburne and Rossetti have done some of their own best poems taking Villon as starting-point. The net result is 'more like Marie de France, Crestien de Troyes, or Froissart'.

I have of sorwe so grete woon[1]
That joye gete I never noon
Now that I see my lady bright
Which I have loved with al my myght
Is fro me deed and is a-goon.[2]

Allas, Deeth, what ayleth thee
That thou noldest[3] have taken me
Whan thou toke my lady sweete
That was so fayr, so fresh, so fre,
So good, that men may wel se
Of al goodnesse she had no meete.[4]

[1] of sorrow great extent   [2] gone   [3] wouldst not   [4] mate, equal

English lyric, the technique for singing already complete,
no augmentation of singability from Chaucer's days to our
own. The French fourteenth-century lyric mode, common
to all Europe. Idiom has changed, but no greater *fitness to
be sung* has been attained. Not even by Shakespeare with
the aid of later Italian song-books.

But as I romed up and doun
I fond that on a walle ther was
Thus written on a table of bras:
I wol now synge, gif that I can
The armes and also the man
That first cam, through his destinee
Fugitif of Troy contree
In Italie . . . . .

Ther saw I how the tempest stente
And how with allé pyne he wente
And prevely took arryvage
In the contree of Cartage
And on the morwe, how that he
And a knyght hight Achaté
Metten with Venus that day
Goyng in a queynt array
As she hadde been an hunteresse
With wynd blowynge upon hir tresse.

Chaucer giving his tentative impression of Virgil.

Chaucer deriving from Latin is possibly bookish. He is better when French, he is greatest in drawing the Pardoner, Wife of Bath and live people, putting often the results of his own READING into their mouths, and drawing *their* character in the way they make use of it. The pardoner takes two hundred lines to get to his story. By that time the reader is very much surprised that he has a story at all.

Chaucer's *observed* characters are perhaps more real to us than Shakespeare's dramatized figures, or come at one more suddenly from the page as living, whereas the actor intervenes, or needs to intervene, to 're-create' the Elizabethan dramatic personage.

This must be taken as a tentative statement, with all grades of faintness and vividness implied.

Hyd, Absalon, thyne gilte tresses clere
Ester, ley thow thy mekenesse al adoun,
Hyde, Jonathas, al thy frendely manere;
Penelope and Marcia Catoun,
Mak of youre wyfhod no comparisoun,
Hyde ye youre beuteis, Ysoude and Elene,
Alceste is here that al that may destene[1]

Thyn fayre body lat it nat apeere,
Laveyne, and thow, Lucresse of Rome town
And Pollexene that boughte love so dere
Ek Cleopatre with al thyn passioun
Hide ye youre trouth in love and youre renoun
And thow Tysbe, that hast for love swich peyne,
Alceste is here that al that may desteyne.

Herro, Dido, Laodamya alle in fere[2]
Ek Phillis hangynge for thyn Demophoun
And Canace espied by thyn chere[3]
Ysiphile betrayed with Jasoun
Mak of youre trouthe in love no bost, ne soun
Nor Ypermystre, or Adriane ne pleyne,
Alceste is here that al that may desteyne.

[1] overshadow   [2] company   [3] face

Provençal tradition, via France, the mediaeval, that
lasted to Villon's time. Cf. Neiges d'Antan; and other
ballades. Villon born over a century after Chaucer, England not lagging behind France.

You do not have to apologize for Chaucer or say that he was an Englishman or only an Englishman, you can cast about in your mind without inhibition when seeking comparisons either for his singableness or for his character drawing.

Where, for example, in anterior literature can you find better or as good?

There is some such drawing in the sagas, less in Boccaccio, less variety in Petronius, if you try to think of something more or less 'like it' you may be reminded of Plato's humour, for example in dealing with the apoplectic army captain (colonel) who is so annoyed with Socrates because the old inquirer's mind happens to function. Pardoner and host do not suffer by comparison. Daphnis and Chloe evinces probably a higher degree of civilization, a more refined but not a more active perception.

There is no need to invent or take for granted a special and specially lenient set of LOCAL criteria when valuing Chaucer.

Collateral reading. **W. S. Landor,** the conversations of Chaucer, Petrarch and Boccaccio.

Lenvoy to King Richard

> O prince desire for to be honourable,
> Cherish thy folk and hate extorcioun!
> Suffre no thing, that may be reprevable
> To thyn estat, don in thy regioun.
> Shew forth thy swerd of castigacioun,
> Dred God, do law, love trouth and worthynesse
> And dryve they folk ageyen to stedfastnesse.

Provençal tradition maintained.

> Thus gan he make a mirrour of his minde
> In which he saw al hoolly[1] her figure,

[1] wholly

Provençal tradition in flower.

Madame ye ben of beaute shryne
As fer as cercled is the mappemounde
For as the cristal glorious ye shyne
And lyke ruby ben your chekes rounde
Therewith ye ben so mery and jocounde
That at revel whan I see you daunce
It is an oyntement unto my wounde,
Though ye to me ne do no daliaunce.

Among the doubtful minor poems we find:

Your yën two wol sleye me sodenly.

That might be by Froissart had he written in English.

Chaucer's work has been left us almost unsorted. The perspicacious reader will not fall to thinking it is all of equal value. Having felt the best, it is probably advisable simply to browse and read what one enjoys; there are parts he might have cut had he been used to the multiplication of books by the printing press; parts that he could have rewritten had he thought it worth while. No good purpose is served by merely falling into an ecstasy over archaic forms of the language.

A rough division might perhaps be tried.

1   Poems magnificently maintaining Provençal tradition.

2   Poems akin to those of his French contemporaries.

3   Passages showing the particular Chaucerian enrichment, or humanity.

4   Inferior passages where he hasn't bothered to do more than a rough translation, or has left ineffective lists, or scuttered over less interesting matter.

Intending writers can read him with fair safety, in so far as no one now can possibly use an imitation of Chaucer's manner or the details of his speech. Whereas horrible examples of people wearing Elizabethan old clothes, project from whole decades of later English and American writing.

The modern writer if he learn from Chaucer can only learn from CHAUCER'S art, its fundamentals.

The question of using another man's manner or 'style' is fairly simple. Good writing is coterminous with the writer's thought, it has the form of the thought, the form of the way the man feels his thought.

No two men think in precisely the same way. Mr. Wyndham Lewis may have an excellent coat, but it would not give sartorial satisfaction on the back of Mr. Joyce, or Mr. Eliot, and so in varying degree, until a writer uses a speech of his own, there will be odd bulges, or a slackness over narrower shoulders.

113

The particular English component is in Chaucer. From now on, the student in computing the later poets and prose writers, can ask himself:

What have they that was not in Don Geoffrey? You can ask this of Shakespeare; you can ask it of Fielding.

The battelis and the man I will discruive
Fra Troyis boundis first that fugitive
By fate to Italie come, and coist Lauyne
Ouer land and se cachit[1] with meikill pyne
Be force of goddis aboue, fra euery stede[2]
Of cruel Juno throw auld remembrit feid[3]
Grete payne in batteles sufferit he also
Or[4] he is goddis brocht in Latio
And belt the ciete, fra quham of nobil fame
The Latyne peopil taken has thare name,
And eike the faderis princis of Alba
Come, and the walleris of grete Rome alsua,
O thow, my muse, declare the causis quhay,[5]
Qyhat maiesty offendit; schaw quham by,
Or zit quharefor, of goddis the drcry[6] Quene.
So feil[7] dangeris, sic trawell maid sustene
Ane worthy man fulfillit of pietie:
Is thare sic greif[8] in heuinlie myndes on hie?

---

[1] chased   [2] stead = place   [3] feud, hatred   [4] Ere   [5] *qu* for *w*
[6] orig. Sax. means *bloody*   [7] *many*   [8] greif, indignation for offence

---

1474 to 1521 or '22.

Gavin Douglas, set on a particular labour, with his mind full of Latin quantitative metre, attains a robuster versification than you are likely to find in Chaucer. It is not fair to compare these particular passages to Chaucer's Virgilian fragments as if Chaucer had done nothing else. But the texture of Gavin's verse is stronger, the resilience greater than Chaucer's.

115

With wappinnis like the Virgins of spartha

. . . . .

For Venus efter the gys and maner thare
Ane active bow, apoun her schulder bare
As sche had bene ane wilde huntereis
With wind waffing hir haris lowsit of trace

. . . . .

And on this wise with hart burning as fyre
Musing alone full of malice and yre
To Eolus cuntre that wyndy regioun
Ane brudy[1] land of furious stormy soun
This goddes went quhare Eolus the King
In gousty cauis[2] the windis loud quhisling
And braithlie tempestis by his power refranys
In bandis hard, schet in presoun constrenys.

[1] fertile   [2] *u* for *v*

The translation was made during the eighteen months,
beginning in January, 1512 and ending on the 22nd of
July 1513, with two months' intermission, the work going
faster as he proceeded, 7th book begun December 1512.

Printed 'at London' by 1553.

Thay vmbeset the seyis bustuously
Quhill fra the depe till euyrye coist fast by
The huge wallis[1] weltres apon hie
Rowit at anis[2] with stormes and wyndis thre
Eurus, Nothus, and the wynd Aphricus
(Quhilk Eist, South and West wyndis hate[3] with us.)
Sone eftir this of men the clamour rais,[4]
The takillis graffillis, cabillis can frate[5] and frais.
With the cloudis, heuynnys son and dayis lycht
Hid and brest out of the Troianis sycht
Derknes as nycht, beset the see about,
The firmament gan[6] rumyllyng rare and rout.
The skyis oft lychtned with fyry leuyn
And schortlie baith are, see and heuyn
And euery thyng manissis the men to de
Schewand the dede present before thare E.

---

[1] waves   [2] Rolled at once   [3] are called   [4] rose
[5] crackle   [6] *gan = began* beat and bang

Go slow, manissis = menaces, the key to most of the
unfamiliar-looking words in the sound. Don't be afraid to
guess. Rare = roar, rout = bellow, E = eye.

'Bishop of Dunkeld and Unkil to the Earl of Angus'

> And all in vain thus quhil Eneas carpit[1]
> Ane blasterend bub[2] out fra the narth braying
> Gan ouer the foreschip in the bak sail ding
> And to the sternes up the flude can cast[3]
> The airi,[4] hatchis and the takillis brast[5]
> The schippis steuyn thrawart hir went can wryith[6]
> And turnit her braid syde to the wallis swyth[7]
> Hie as ane hill the jaw of the watter brak

---

[1] carped [2] blustering storm [3] (old ships higher at stern)
[4] oars [5] burst
[6] ? also technical nautical *ware* 'faire virer', cause to turn. Possibly a textual error, I don't make out whether the ship's stem, main keel timber twists forward, i.e. wryd or wrything loose from the ribs, or whether it is merely a twisted forward lurch of the ship [7] quickly

---

I am no great shakes as a Latinist, but I do read Latin for pleasure, and have read a good deal, and have possibly brought to light several qualities of Propertius' writing which the professional Latinists had ignored, and in such passages as this I get considerably more pleasure from the Bishop of Dunkeld than from the original highly cultured but non-seafaring author.

. . . . .

The religious woman quham thay socht
Baith consecrate to Diane and Phebus
Hait[1] Deiphebe, the douchter of Glaucus,
Quhilk to the King sone spake apoun this wise:
    This time (quod sche) to stare and to deuise
Gouand[2] on figuris, is not necessary.
Mare needful now it war but[3] langare tary
Seuin zoung[4] stottis[5] that zoik[6] bare neuer nane
Brocht from the bowe[7] in offerand brittin[8] ilkane
And als mony twynteris,[9] as is the gise
Chosin and ganand[10] for the sacrifice.
    On this wise till Eneas spak Sibyll.

GAVIN DOUGLAS 1474–1522

All the midway is wildernes unplane
Or wilsum forrest and the laithlie flude
Cocytus with his drery bosum unrude[11]
Flowis enuiroun round about that place
Bot gif fa grete desire and luf thou has
Twyis til owre sale[12] of Styx the dolly[13] lake
And twyis behald blak hellis pit of wrake,[14]
Or fa huge laubour delitis the, quod scho,
Harkin quhat first behuffis the to do.
Amiddis ane rank tre, lurkis a goldin beuch[15]
With aureate leuis and flexibil twistis teuch,[16]

---

[1] Named   [2] Gazing   [3] without   [4] *z* for *y*   [5] bullocks
[6] yoke   [7] cow-fold   [8] break in offering = sacrifice
[9] sheep 'two winters' old   [10] propitious (gagnant)
[11] the *un* intensive not negative   [12] ? hall, or sailing place
[13] dolorous   [14] revenge
[15] My glossary gives *beuch* = *bough*, but bush would imply that
Gavin took it for mistletoe   [16] tough

Unto Juno infernale consecrate,

That standis loukit[1] about and obumbrate

With dirk schaddois of the thik wod schaw.

Bot it is na wyse lesum,[2] I the schaw

Thir secrete wayis under the erd to went

Quhil of the tre this goldin grane[3] be rent:

Fare Proserpyne has institute and command

To offer hir this hir awin proper presand.[4]

Ane uthir goldin grane, to the ilk effeck,

Thou sall not mys, thocht the first be doun brek,

Incontinent euer of the samyn metal

Sic ane like branche sal burgeoun furth withal.

The nedis, therefor, til hald thine ene on hicht

It for to serche and seik al at richt.

Quhen it is fund, thou hynt[5] it in thy hand

For gif it list, esely that samyn wand

Of the awin[6] wil sal follow thi grip fute hate[7]

Gif so the fatis will thou pas that gate;

Or elles[8] be na strenth thou sal it ryffe[8]

Nor cut in twa with wappin, swerde nor knyfe.

[1] enclosed   [2] lawful, permitted

[3] the glossary now gives *bough*, *grain*, the latter certainly the more likely, and again pointing to Gavin's having the mistletoe in mind. The glose-maker possibly thinking more of the original Latin than of the word before him?   [4] present   [5] snatch

[6] its own   [7] Chaucer, foothot = straight-way

[8] divination according to whether the bough comes off easily

---

The omission of Douglas from *The Oxford Book of XVIth Century Verse* sheds no credit on either the press or their anthologist. Blind prejudice against translation cannot explain it, as Douglas wrote a quantity of original poetry, part of which is indubitably superior to a good deal they have included.

Behaldand the large wod on athir syde:
Thare as he stude thus makand his prayer:
Wald God zone goldin branche list now appere

. . . . .

Skars war thir wordis said, quhen in that place
Ane pair of dowis fra heuin come with ane flycht
And richt forgane the mannis face did lycht

. . . . .

This rial prince als sone as he thaym saw
His moderis birdis knew, and blythlie than
His vrisoun[1] has maid and thus began:
    O haly foulis, gif the way may be went,
Be ze my gidis to complete my entent;
Addres zour cours throwout the are in hy
Unto that haly schaw[2] . . . . .

And ze my blissit moder that oure beild[3] is
Into this doutsum cais. . . .

---

[1] orison   [2] grove
[3] glossary gives *refuge*, *help*, but I think it is more likely to be *bail surety*

Distinguish between Virgil's new matter, that is the folk-lore that is distinctly Italian, not Greek, and the parts of the Aeneid due to literary tradition.

Like as full oft in schil[1] wynteris tyde
The gum or glew[2] amyd the woddis wyde
Is wount to schene zallow[3] on the grane new[4]
Quhilk never of that treis substance grew
With saffroun hewit[5] frute doing furth sproute
Cirkillis[6] and wympillis[7] round bewis about
Sic lik was of this gold the cullour brycht
That burgeonit fare on the rank aikis[8] hicht
Euer as the branche for pipand wynd reboundit,
The golden schakeris[9] ratlis and resoundit.
Eneas smertlie hynt the grane that schone
And but[10] delay has rent it doun anone.

Gavin Douglas 1474–1522

Enee hymself ane zow was blak of fleece
Brytnit[11] with his swerd in sacrifice ful hie
Unto the moder of the furies thre
And hir grete sister, and to Proserpyne
Ane zeld[12] kow all to trinschit, and eftir syne
To the infernale King, quhilk Pluto hate,[13]
Hys nycht altaris begouth[14] to dedicate
The haile boukis of beistis bane and lyre[15]
Amyd the flambis keist[16] and haly fyre
The fat olye did he zet and pere[17]
Apoun the entrellis to mak thaym birne clere.

[1] chill   [2] gum, viscous humour   [3] yellow   [4] newly
[5] hued   [6] circles and kinks   [7] around the boughs   [8] oak's
[9] skakers, labels, thin plates of gold rattled   [10] without
[11] ASax brytan = break, kill, sacrifice   [12] barren, hacked
[13] hyght = is called   [14] began
[15] The holy bulks (carcasses) of beasts, bone and flesh   [16] cast
[17] poured

Suffers nothing if compared to witch passages in *Macbeth*.

The byisning beist the serpent Lerna
Horribill quhissilland, and queynt Chimera,
With fire enarmyt on hir toppis hie,
The laithlye Harpies, and the Gorgonis thre
Of thrinfald bodyis, gaistly formes did grone
Baith of Erylus and of Gerione.

.　.　.　.　.

And with his bitand brycht brand all in vane
The tume[1] schaddois smityng to have slane.

.　.　.　.　.

Awounderit of this sterage and the preis,
Say me, virgine, sayd Enee, or thou ceis,
Quhat menis sic confluence on this wattir syde?
Quhat wald thir saulis? quhay will they not abyde?

.　.　.　.　.

The tothir ansueris with ane pietuous pepe,
Maist wourthy Duke, Anchises' son maist dere

.　.　.　.　.

The helmstok or gubernakil of tre
Quharewith I rewlit our cours throw the se
Lenand thereon sa fast, percase it threw
And rent away ouerburd with me I drew.
The wally seyis to witnes draw I here
That for myself tuke I nane sa grete fere
As of thy schip.

[1] empty

A note which I take to be Gavin's own indicates the
debt to Homer; as those who do not read Latin can get
their Virgil in olde Scots, the Romans who knew no Greek
got their legend of the NEKUIA from Virgil.

The God now having laide aside his
  borrowed shape of Bull,
Had in his likenesse showed himself:
  And with his pretie trull
Tane landing in the Isle of Crete.
  When in that while her Sire
Not knowing where she was become, sent after
  to enquire
Hir brother Cadmus,   charging him his sister
  home to bring,
Or never for to come againe: wherein he
  did a thing
For which he might both justlie kinde and cruel
  called be.
When Cadmus over all the world had saught
  (for who is hee
That can detect the thefts of Jove)   and no-
  where could her see:
Then as an outlaw (to avoyde his father's
  wrongful yre)
He went to Phebus Oracle   most humbly to
  desire
His heavenly council,   where he would assigne
  him place to dwell.
                       . . . . .
                       . . . . .

An olde forgrowne unfelled wood stood near at
  hand thereby
And in the middes a queachie plot with Sedge
  and Oysiers hie.

Where courbde about with peble stone   in
   likenesse of a bow
There was a spring with silver streames   that
   forth thereof did flow.
Here lurked in his lowring den God Mars his
   griesly Snake
With golden scales and firie eyes beswolne with
   poyson blake.
Three spirting tongues,   three rowes of teeth
   within his head did sticke.
No sooner had the Tirian folke set foote within
   this thicke
And queachie plot,   and deped down their
   bucket in the well,
But that to buscle in his den began this Serpent fell
And peering with a marble[1] head right horribly
   to hisse.
    . . . . .

   The specled serpent straight
Comes trailing out in waving linkes and knottie
   rolles of scales,
And bending into bunchie boughts his bodie forth
   he hales.
And lifting up above the wast   himself unto
   the Skie
He overlooketh all the wood;
    . . . . .

    With that he raughting fast
A mightie Milstone,   at the Snake with all
   his might it cast.
    . . . . .

[1] marbled

While Cadmus wondered at the hugenesse of the
    vanquisht foe,
Upon the sodaine came a voyce: from whence
    he could not know.
But sure he was he heard the voyce, which said:
    Agenor's sonne,
What gazest thus upon this Snake?   The
    time will one day come
That thou thy selfe shalt ba a Snake.   He
    pale and wan for feare
Had lost his speech: and ruffled up   stiffe
    staring stood his heare.
Behold (mans helper at his neede) Dame Pallas
    gliding through
The vacant Ayre   was straight at hand and
    bade him take a plough
And cast the Serpents teeth in ground   as of
    the which should spring
Another people out of hand.

       . . . . .

             the clods began to move
And from the forrow first of all the pikes ap-
    pearde above,
Next rose up helmes with fethered crests, and
    then the Poldrens bright,
Successively the Curets whole and all the armour
    right.
Thus grew up men like corne in field in rankes of
    battle ray

I apologize for the cuts in the story, but I cannot give a
whole book of the Metamorphoses here, and I do not

honestly think that anyone can know anything about the art of lucid narrative in English, or let us say about the history of the development of English narrative-writing (verse or prose) without seeing the whole of the volume ('The xv Bookes of P. Ouidius Naso, entytuled Metamorphosis, translated oute of Latin into English meeter, by Arthur Golding Gentleman.' First edition, so far as I know, Imprinted at London by Willyam Seres, 1567, with the mark of bear standing at post inside the garter. Honi soit). Shakespeare, b. 1564, d. 1616.

Though it is the most beautiful book in the language, I am not here citing it for decorative purposes but for the narrative quality.

It should be read as natural spoken language. The metre is, I admit, susceptible to bad reading. A bad reader of fourteeners is almost certain to tub-thump. The reader will be well advised to read according to sense and syntax, keep from thumping, observe the syntactical pause, and not stop for the line ends save where sense requires or a comma indicates. That is the way to get the most out of it, and come nearest to a sense of the time-element in the metrical plan.

Their tales did ende and Mineus daughters still
    their businesse plie
In spight of Bacchus   whose high feast they
    breəke contemptuously.
When   on the sodaine (seeing naught)   they
    heard about them round
Of tubbish Timbrels perfectly a hoarse and
    jarring sound
With shraming shalmes   and gingling belles
    and furthermore they felt
A cent of Saffron   and of Myrrhe   that verie
    hotly smelt
And   (which a man would ill believe)   the
    web they had begun
Immediately waxt freshe and greene,   the
    flaxe the which they spun
Did flourish full of Ivie leaves.   And part
    thereof did run
Abrode in Vines.   The threede it selfe in
    braunches forth did spring.
Young burgeons   full of clustred grapes
    their Distaves forth did bring
And as the web they wrought was dey'd a deep
    darke purple hew,
Even so   upon the painted grapes   the
    selfe same colour grew.

The day was spent. And now was come the
    tyme   which neyther night

Nor day, but middle bound of both   a man
    may terme of right.
The house at sodaine seemed to shake,   and all
    about it shine
With burning lampes,   and glittering fires to
    flash before their eyen.
And likenesses of ougly beastes with gastful
    noyses yeld.
For feare whereof   in smokie holes the sisters
    were compeld
To hide their heades,   one here and there
    another for to shun
The glistering light. And while they thus in
    corners blindly run,
Upon their little pretie limmes   a fine crispe
    filme there goes
And slender finnes   instead of handes   their
    shortened armes enclose.
But how they lost their former shape   of
    certaintie to know
The darknesse would not suffer them.   No
    feathers on them grow
And yet with shere and vellume wings they hover
    from the ground
And when they goe about to speake   they
    make but little sound
According as their bodies give bewayling their
    despight
By chirping shrilly to themselves.   In houses
    they delight
And not in woodes: detesting day   they
    flitter towards night

Wherethrough they of the Evening late in Latin
  take their name
And we in English language Backes or Reermice
  call the same.

. . . . .

. . . . .

Now while I underneath the Earth the Lake of
  Styx did passe
I saw your daughter Proserpine with these same
  eyes. She was
Not merie,   neyther rid of feare as seemed by
  hir cheere
But yet a Queene,   but yet of great God Dis
  the stately Feere:[1]
But yet of that same droupie Realme the chiefe
  and sovereigne Peere.

. . . . .

. . . . .

And came of mightie Marsis race,   Pandion
  sought of joyne
Aliance with him by and by,   and gave him to
  his Feere
His daughter Progne.   At this match   (as
  after will appeare)
Was neither Juno, President of mariage, wont
  to bee
Nor Hymen,   no   nor any one of all the
  graces three.

[1] companion

130

The Furies   snatching Tapers up that on some
    Herse did stande,
Did light them,   and before the Bride did
    beare them in their hande.

. . . . .

. . . . .

As both Progne and hir selfe should joy and
    confort bring,
When both of them in verie deede should after-
    ward it rew.
To endward of his daily race and travell Phoebus
    drew
And on the shoring side of Heaven his horses
    downeward flew.

. . . . .

In open face of all the world: or if thou keepe
    me still
As prisoner in these woods,   my voyce the
    verie woods shall fill
And make the stones to understand.

. . . . .

The student will note that up to now the writers exhibited are all intent on what they are saying, they are all
conscious of having something to tell the reader, something
he does not *already know*, and their main effort is spent in
TELLING him.

The next phase appears in authors who are gradually
more and more concerned with the way they are saying it.

. . . . .

131

Similar change in painting: Simone Memmi, the painters of the Quattrocento, intent on their MAIN subject, Virgin sitting on bed with child, etc., unity in picture. Renaissance decadence: painters intent on painting a bit of drapery, this or that bit of a picture, or chiaroscuro or what not.

Contrast

Chaucer   Shakespeare
the European.   the Englishman.

FOUR PERIODS

I. When England was part of Europe.

II. When England was England, containing her own best writers, her own most intelligent men.

III. The period when England no longer had room for, or welcomed her best writers.

> Landor in Italy.
>
> Beddoes in Germany.
>
> Byron, Keats, Shelley in Italy.
>
> Browning in Italy, Tennyson the official literature of England.

IV. The period of exotic injection.

As distinct from the classic tradition, Latin had belonged to all Europe. There are various flows of Latinization in English, but the 'injection' is something different.

Wordsworth and Shelley were both conscious of importing Italian canzone forms.

Swinburne: Greek injection.

Browning, in a different way, uses Italian subject matter. Fitzgerald's *Rubaiyat* (Persian).

Wm. Morris: Norse sagas, and old French matter.

Rossetti: Italian poets. Pre-Raphaelite mediaevalism. Victorian minor fiddling with slighter French forms.

The 'Celtic': i.e. French symboliste tendencies mixed with subject matter first from Celtic myth, then from modern Ireland.

The American colonization: Henry James (Whistler, W. H. Hudson), etc.

Fra bank to bank, fra wood to wood I rin
Ourhailit with my feeble fantasie
Like til a leaf that fallis from a tree
Or til a reed ourblawin with the wind,

Two gods guides me, the ane of them is blin,
Yea, and a bairn brocht up in vanitie,
The next a wife ingenrit of the sea
And lichter nor a dauphin with her fin.

Unhappy is the man for evermair
That tills the sand and sawis in the air,

But twice unhappier is he, I lairn,
That feidis in his heart a mad desire
And follows on a woman throw the fire
Led by a blind and teachit by a bairn.

Sonnet properly divided in octave and sestet. There is in Perugia a painting of Christ emerging from the tomb; one sees what Perugino was trying to do, and how he was endeavouring to improve on his predecessors. These works of perfect ripeness often have nothing wrong in themselves, and yet serve as points from which we can measure a decadence.

Boyd is 'saying it in a beautiful way'.

The apple is excellent for a few days or a week before it is ripe, then it is ripe; it is still excellent for a few days after it has passed the point of maturity.

I suppose this is the most beautiful sonnet in the language, at any rate it has one nomination.

Now on the sea from her olde loue comes shee
That drawes the day from heaven's cold axle-tree,
Aurora whither slidest thou down againe,
And brydes from Memnon yeerly shall be slaine.

Now in her tender arms I sweetlie bide,
If ever, now well lies she by my side,
The ayre is colde and sleep is sweetest now
And byrdes send foorth shrill notes from every bow.
Whither runst thou, that men and women loue not?
Holde in thy rosie horses that they moue not!
Ere thou rise, stars teach seamen where to saile
But when thou comest, they of their courses faile.
Poore trauilers though tired rise at thy sight,
The painful[1] Hinde by thee to fild is sent,
Slow oxen early in the yoke are pent,
Thou cousenest boys of sleep and dost betray them
To Pedants that with cruel lashes pay them.

[1] Fr. cf. *homme de peine*, one who must work

The apex, period of maximum power in English versification, the vigour full and unspent, the full effect of study of
Latin metre. The Elizabethan age was concerned with this
problem. The men who tried to fit English to rules they
found in Latin grammarians have been largely forgotten,
but the men who filled their minds with the feel of the
Latin have left us the deathless criteria.

Marlowe's version of Ovid's Amores, printed in HOL-
LAND, Puritan pest already beginning.

The lay reader can use these exhibits as signposts for further reading. Where the book is used for class work, the teacher will naturally make his own additions and amplifications from easily obtainable texts, or pick the sound work from the general welter of mediocre performance exhibited in the current anthologies where the best is often obscured. I take it that texts of Shakespeare, Marlowe, FitzGerald's Omar are so easily obtainable as to make it needless to print selections from them in this brief book, and that the traditional miscellanies copied one from another with no critical plan, small honesty, and almost no personal estimate, or re-examination of their matter, contain fair testimony as to the value of many writers of short poems, 'lyrics', etc., and that this section entitled exhibits serves, you might say, to trace the course of English poesy, and to indicate in a general way the 'development' or at any rate the transmutation of style in the writing of verse.

I have pointed out in a longer essay, that one could almost trace the changes in British manner without wider reading than the series of attempts to give an English version of Horace.

THE ECSTASY

Where like a pillow on a bed
A pregnant bank swell'd up to rest
The violet's reclining head
Sat we two, one another's best.

Our hands were firmly cémented
By a fast balm which thence did spring,
Our eye-beams twisted and did thread
Our eyes upon one double string

So to engraft our hands, as yet
Was all the means to make us one,
And pictures in our eyes to get
Was all our propagation.

As twixt two equal armies Fate
Suspends uncertain victory,
Our souls, which to advance their state
Were gone out, hung twixt her and me.

And whilst our souls negotiate there,
We like sepulchral statues lay.
All day the same our postures were
And we said nothing all the day.

If any, so by love refined
That he soul's language understood
And by good love were grown all mind,
Within convenient distance stood,

137

He, though he knew not which soul spake
(Because both meant, both spoke the same),
Might thence a new concoction[1] take
And part far purer than he came.

This ecstasy doth unperplex,
We said, and tell us what we love,
We see by this it was not sex
We see, we saw not what did move,

But as all several souls contain
Mixture of things they know not what,
Love these mixed souls doth mix again
And make both one, each this and that.

A single violet transplant,
The strength, the colour and the size,
All, which before was poor and scant,
Redoubles still and multiplies,

When love with one another so
Interinanimates two souls
That abler soul which thence doth flow
Defects of loneliness controls,

We then, who are this new soul, know
Of what we are composed and made,
For th' anatomies of which we grow
Are souls whom no change can invade.

[1] Technical alchemical term

But O alas, so long, so far
Our bodies why do we forbear?
They are ours though they're not we. We are
Th' intelligences, they the spheres.

We owe them thanks because they thus
Did us to us at first convey;
Yielded their forces to us
Nor are dross to us, but allay.[1]

On man heaven's influence works not so
But that it first imprints the air,
So soul into soul may flow
Though it to body first repair

As our blood labours to beget
Spirits as like souls as it can
Because such fingers need to knit
That subtle knot which makes us man

So must pure lovers' souls descend
To affections and to faculties
Which sense may reach and apprehend
Else a great prince in prison lies.

To our bodies turn we then that so
Weak men on love reveal'd may look,
Loves mysteries in souls do grow
But yet the body is his book

[1] alloy, i.e. that makes metal fit for a given purpose

And if some lover such as we
Have heard this dialogue of one,
Let him still mark us, he shall see
Small change when we're to bodies[1] gone.

[1] probably technical for atoms.

Platonism believed. The decadence of trying to make pretty speeches and of hunting for something to say, temporarily checked. Absolute belief in the existence of an extra-corporeal soul, and its incarnation, Donne stating a thesis in precise and even technical terms. Trivial half-wits always looking for the irrelevant, boggle over Donne's language. You have here a clear statement, worthy to set beside Cavalcanti's 'Donna mi Prega' for its precision, less interesting metrically, but certainly not less interesting in content.

It would take a bile specialist to discover why the *Oxford Book of Verse* includes the first five of the strophes and then truncates the poem with *no indication that anything has been omitted.*

Donne's work is uneven, there is a great deal of it, but he is the one English metaphysical poet who towers above all the rest. This doesn't mean there weren't other learned and convinced Platonists who have left beautiful poems. Neither does it mean that Donne at his lowest potential doesn't march coterminous with his dallying contemporaries.

In Donne's best work we 'find again' a real author saying something he means and not simply 'hunting for sentiments that will fit his vocabulary'.

It might be well to emphasize the difference between an expert and inexpert metaphysician. For centuries a series

140

of men thought very thoroughly and intently about certain problems which we find unsusceptible to laboratory proof and experiment. The results of such thinking can be known and compared, gross follies and self-contradiction can be eliminated. The difference between a metaphysical treatise that could satisfy my late friend, the Father José Maria de Elizondo, and contemporary religious works whose authors cite Mr. Wells and Mr. Balfour, is very considerable.

Equations of psychology worked out by knowers of Avicenna may not be wholly convincing, but a number of such equations exist, and cannot be disproved by experience, even though belief and predilection must depend on the introspective analysis of highly sensitized persons.

Between 1250 and the Renaissance, people did manage to communicate with each other in respect to such perceptions and such modalities of feeling and perception.

Violets

Welcome, maids of honour,
    You do bring
    In the Spring
And wait upon her.

She has virgins many,
    Fresh and fair;
    Yet you are
More sweet than any.

You're the maiden posies
    And so graced
    To be placed
'Fore damask roses.

Yet, though thus respected,
    By-and-by
    Ye do die,
Poor girls, neglected.

By comparison with troubadours the rhyming is infantile. That does not mean that a maximum of singability is unattained.

The number of rhymes that can be used to advantage in one language is NOT the numerical measure for any other.

In an inflected language like Latin there is such a frequency of *-um*-arum,-orum and *-abat* that identical sounds would be intolerable if they were stuck into prominence, or repeated at regular instead of irregular intervals.

Rhyming can be used to zone sounds, as stones are heaped into walls in mountain ploughland.

Verses of probably no literary value, but illustrating a kind of rhythm, a melodic innovation that you will not find in Chaucer, though there is ample precedence in Provence.

In the case of the madrigal writers the words were not published apart from the music in their own day, and one supposes that only a long-eared, furry-eared epoch would have thought of printing them apart from their tunes as has been done in our time.

We observe that William Young's music has just been edited by Dr. Whittaker and that John Jenkins was still in MSS. on January 1, 1934.

Herrick, as you observe, lived to a ripe old age. It is unlikely that the above brief mouthful of melody was an early effort.

EXERCISE

I Let the student try to decide whether there are 100 good poems in whatever general anthology he possesses; or fifty, or thirty.

II How many of the poems he first thinks of will be poems having one good line, or two or three lines that stick in the memory, but which he will have great difficulty in reading to the end, or from which he can remember nothing save the pleasing line?

III How often will he remember a line and be utterly unable to remember the subject of the poem as a whole?

IV Do the following poems:

The early Alisoun, Walsinghame, Wyatt's 'They flee from me', Peele's 'Batsabe sings', Henry VIII's 'Pastime and good company', contain any element not represented in the present set of 'exhibits'.

V Let the student hunt for a dozen poems that are different from any of the exhibits, or that introduce some new component, or enlarge his conception of poetry, by bringing in some kind of matter, or mode of expression not yet touched on.

Were I (who to my cost already am
One of those strange prodigious Creatures, Man)
A Spirit, free to choose for my own share, ⎫
What sort of Flesh and Blood I pleas'd to wear, ⎬
I'd be a Dog, a Monkey, or a Bear, ⎭
Or anything but that vain Animal,
Who is so proud of being Rational.

The modest editor of the Tonson, 1696, edition contents himself with a six-page preface, and for the sake of comparison gives Boileau's fourteen lines,

> A Monsieur M . . . . .
> Docteur de SORB;

Oldham's English version which runs to seventeen, and the above by Rochester with the observation that: 'It might vex a patient Reader, shou'd I go about very minutely to shew the difference here betwixt these two Authors, tis sufficient to set them together.'

I cite this preface to show that intelligent criticism is not my personal invention. God's apes like B. d S., X.Z.Q.K., etc., hadn't the excuse of there not having been a decent English criticism or enlightened modes of estimation for them to learn from. When the style of a period is good, it will probably be possible to discover that good writers had an educated periphery capable of knowing eagle from buzzard.

To His Sacred MAJESTY On His Restoration.

Vertues triumphant Shrine! who do'st engage
At once three Kingdoms in a Pilgrimage;
Which in extatic Duty strive to come
Out of themselves, as well as from their home:
Whilst *England* grows one Camp, and *London* is
It self the Nation, not Metropolis;
And Loyal *Kent* renews her Arts agen,
Fencing her ways with moving Groves of Men;
Forgive this distant Homage, which does meet
Your blest approach on sedentary feet:

And though my Youth, not patient yet to bear
The weight of Arms, denies me to appear
In steel before you, yet, Great SIR, approve
My Manly Wishes, and more vigorous Love;
In whom a cold Respect were Treason to
A Father's Ashes, greater than to You;
Whose one Ambition 'tis for to be known
By daring Loyalty your *Wilmot*'s Son.

A PASTORAL In Imitation of the Greek of Moschus
Bewailing the Death of the Earl of Rochester.

Mourn, all ye Groves, in darker Shades be seen,
Let Groans be heard where gentle Winds have been:
Ye *Albion* Rivers, weep your Fountains dry,
And all ye Plants your Moisture spend and die:
Ye melancholy Flowers, which once were Men,
Lament, until you be transform'd agen,
Let every Rose pale as the Lily be,
And Winter Frost seize the Anemone:
But thou, O *Hyacinth*, more vigorous grow,   ⎫
In mournful Letters thy sad Glory show,   ⎬
Enlarge thy Grief, and flourish in thy Woe:⎭
For *Bion*, the beloved *Bion*'s dead,
His Voice is gone, his tuneful Breath is fled.

Come, all ye Muses, *come, adorn the
Shepherd's Herse,
With never-fading Garlands, never-
dying Verse.*

The first effort of misguided ink-page scholars would be
to FIND THE AUTHOR. Note that the author particularly refrained from signing the poem. As the great mediaeval architects and stone-cutters refrained from signing
their work. One of the great maladies of modern criticism
is this first rush to look for the person, and the correspon·
ding failure EVER to look *at* the thing.

Mourn, ye sweet Nightengales in the thick Woods,
Tell the sad News to all the *British* Floods:
See it to *Isis* and to *Cham* convey'd,
To *Thames*, to *Humber*, and to utmost *Tweed*:
And bid them waft the bitter Tidings on,
How *Bion's* dead, how the lov'd Swain is gone,
And with him all the Art of graceful Song.

> *Come, all ye* MUSES, *come, adorn the Shepherd's Herse,*
> *With never-fading Garlands, never-dying Verse.*

Ye gentle Swans, that haunt the Brooks and Springs,
Pine with sad Grief, and droop your sickly Wings:
In doleful Notes the heavy Loss bewail;
Such as you sing at your own Funeral,
Such as you sung when your lov'd *Orpheus* fell.
Tell it to all the Rivers, Hills, and Plains,
Tell it to all the *British* Nymphs and Swains,
And bid them too the dismal Tydings spread,
Of *Bion's* fate, of *England's Orpheus* dead.

> *Come, all ye* MUSES, *come, adorn the Shepherd's Herse,*
> *With never-fading Garlands, never-dying Verse.*

No more, alas, no more that lovely Swain
Charms with his tuneful Pipe the wondering Plain:

Ceast are those Lays, ceast are those sprightly Ayres,
That woo'd our Souls into our ravish'd Ears:
For which the list'ning Streams forgot to run,
And Trees lean'd their attentive Branches down:
While the glad Hills loth the sweet Sounds to lose,
Lengthen'd in Echoes ev'ry heav'nly close.
Down to the melancholy Shades he's gone,
And there to *Lethe's* Banks reports his moan:
Nothing is heard upon the Mountains now,
But pensive Herds that for their Master lowe:
Stragling and comfortless about they rove,
Unmindful of their Pasture, and their Love.

Come, all ye MUSES, *come, adorn the Shepherd's Herse,
With never-fading Garlands, never-dying Verse.*

. . . . .
. . . . .

Whom has thou left behind thee, skilful Swain,
That dares aspire to reach thy matchless Strain?
Who is there after thee, that dares pretend
Rashly to take thy warbling Pipe in hand?
Thy Notes remain yet fresh in ev'ry Ear,
And give us all Delight, and all Despair:
Pleas'd *Eccho* still does on them meditate,
And to the whistling Reeds their sounds repeat;
Pan only e'er can equal thee in Song,
That task does only to great *Pan* belong:

But *Pan* himself perhaps will fear to try,
Will fear perhaps to be out-done by thee.

Come, all ye MUSES, *come, adorn the*
Shepherd's Herse,
With never-fading Garlands, never-
dying Verse.

Fair *Galatea* too laments thy Death,
Laments the ceasing of thy tuneful Breath:
Oft she, kind Nymph, resorted heretofore
To hear thy artful Measures from the shore:
Nor harsh like the rude Cyclops' were thy Lays,
Whose grating Sounds did her soft Ears displease:
Such was the force of thy enchanting Tongue,
That she for ever could have heard thy Song,
And chid the Hours that do so swiftly run,
And thought the Sun too hasty to go down,
Now does that lovely *Nereid* for thy sake
The Sea, and all her Fellow-*Nymphs* forsake.
Pensive upon the Beech, she sits alone,
And kindly tends the Flocks from which thou'rt gone.

Come, all ye MUSES, *come, adorn the*
Shepherd's Herse,
With never-fading Garlands, never-
dying Verse.

and so on to fifteen pages.

Applied ornament? A few bits of ornament applied by Pietro Lombardo in Santa Maria dei Miracoli (Venice) are worth far more than all the sculpture and 'sculptural creations' produced in Italy between 1600 and 1950.

Rococo, by to-morrow you may be unable to remember a line of it BUT try to find in English another passage of melody sustained for so long, i.e., verse to SING. I have given only six strophes, the elegy runs on for fifteen pages. You can hardly read it without singing, there is no let up in the cantabile quality unless it be in one strophe containing a condensed history of British poetry.

The writer has more difficulty in stopping than in continuing to sing. It is with difficulty that he finds a conclusion.

Compare it with the regular star performance of Spenser's that you can find in any anthology:

Sweet Thames, run softly till I end my song.

By comparison the Spenser is declamatory, that is, to be spoken rhetorically rather than sung. You will find it very hard to make a satisfactory tune for his poem. It sings along, and then there is a clog.

The present verses wouldn't serve a nineteenth-century composer, nor a composer of the first decades of the twentieth. They constrain one to music of the type of their time.

Dowland, Lawes, Young, Jenkins, the period of England's musicianship.

The advantages of having decent musicians ought to be apparent. This composition is not *reading* matter, it is singing matter. Try to find another verbal manifestation that will permit one to make music for half an hour in order to set it.

I refrain from indicating the chief device here employed to induce clear melody. The student should find it for himself.

He can only find it by listening and looking. If he can't find it for himself no amount of telling will make him understand it. There is a single clear principle employed.

It has been perceived that French verse went soggy and leaden, and that it tumefied when some literary lump was too dull to finger the lute; too inarticulate in the basic sense of the word. It is not a man's fingers that stop him playing an instrument but his mind, his inability to grasp mentally the sixty or the twelve or six hundred bits of a whole, and to perceive their relations. The true imagination, whether visual or acoustic, holds a piece of music as a watchmaker would mentally grasp a watch. The 'dull and speechless tribe' or the 'inarticulate' man has only an undifferentiated dumpling, a general sense of there being a certain mass or bulk of something or other before him.

The value of music as elucidation of verse comes from the attention it throws on to the detail. Every popular song has at least one line or sentence that is perfectly clear. This line FITS THE MUSIC. It has usually formed the music.

Pope falls back into the very faults of Boileau which Rochester had purged. The writer does this, not the singer.

Look once more at our anonymous elegy: it is song. Note how few useless words there are in it.

Try the same test on any *writer's* poem. On any set of couplets written in a garret by an unmusical man, whose friends weren't in the habit of playing good music.

We now come upon a

SOCIAL AND ECONOMIC PROBLEM

ADVANTAGES ACCRUING FROM THERE BEING A 'STYLE OF THE PERIOD'

Ils n'existent pas, leur ambience leur confert une existence.

No social order will make a draughtsman like Picasso.

Note (a recent bureaucrat has run up a flag banning cubists and thereby shown himself unfit to conduct a post card emporium).

But the use of having a 'style of the period' *ought* to be apparent both from our anonymous elegy and from Rochester's 'Welcome to Charles', written at the age of twelve.

Both of these poems are made by 'known process'. Their writers didn't have to start by reforming anything.

The musical criteria of the times were of prime order.

Waller, who was a tiresome fellow, is probably telling the truth when he says that his poems were made for his own pleasure and that of his friends, and that he only published them when (or because?) bad copies had been rushed into print without his having seen them.

His natural talent is fathoms below My Lord Rochester's.

BUT when he writes for music he is 'lifted'; he was very possibly HOISTED either by the composer or by the general musical perceptivity of the time and of his acquaintances. His inborn lack of melody, if you compare it with Rochester's, is emended. And he pays his debt in the quite imperfect poem to Lawes.

> Verse makes Heroick Virtue live
> But you can Life to Verses give.
>
> . . . . .
>
> You, by the help of Tune and Time
> Can make that Song which was but Rhime.
> Noy[1] pleading, no man doubts the Cause,
> Or questions verses set by Lawes.
> As a Church-window, thick with paint,
> Lets in a Light but dim and faint,
> So others, with Division, hide
> The light of Sense,
> But you alone may truly boast
> That not a syllable is lost;
>
> The Writer's, and the Setter's, Skill
> At once the ravish'd ears do fill.
> Let those which only warble long
> And gargle in their Throats a Song,
> Content themselves with   UT,   RE,   MI;
> Let words and sense be set by thee.

[1] an advocate

It might be noted in passing that while Lawes set 'Go lovely Rose' he did not, so far as I know, bother with the above bit of first criticism wherefrom I have omitted several but not all of its encumbrances.

Note—on the state of the times.

'. . . that in the midst of their Discourse a Servant has come in to tell him that such and such attended; upon which *Cromwell* would rise, and stop them, talking at the Door, where he would overhear him say, *The Lord will reveal, The Lord will help*, and several such Expressions; which when he return'd to Mr. *Waller* he excus'd, saying *Cousin* Waller, *I must talk to these Men after their own Way.*'

Campion set his own words. Lawes, not content with what he found in English, set, if I remember rightly, a number of Greek and Latin poems.

Thus illustrating the advantage the arts may take from a society having a focus. In an age of musical imbecility we find the aspiring poet in his garret, he never goes to a concert either from lack of curiosity, or because he can't afford to buy concert tickets, that being the fault of a carious and wholly filthy system of economics, but in any case the level of general culture is so low that the poet's impecunious friends are not musicians, or are accustomed only to an agglutinous or banal substitute for good melody.

Poetry AND music from Henry the Eighth's time down to fat Anne's were very generally an accomplishment. I use the singular, because they were so often united.

No one approach has all the advantages.

Rochester IMPROVES on Boileau by his English version, but he does not improve on Seneca's for which only severe intellectual application such as Donne's could have fitted him.

But, as you can see from an exhibit shown later out of its chronological order, there is nothing as good as Rochester, even when he is not writing lyrics, until . . .? (Let the student determine when.)

In all this matter the sonnet is the *devil*. Already by 1300 the Italian sonnet was becoming, indeed had become, declamatory, first because of its having all its lines the same length, which was itself a result of divorce from song.

The art of song, the Provençal art, sublimated by Sordello, stiffens when you get an habitual form. The sonnet was next used for letter writing, used for anything not needing a new tune perforce for every new poem.

You had to have a new tune when the strophes of each poem were different from those of any other, or were else regarded as plagiarism, or frankly sung to the precedent music and definitely labelled 'Sirventes', a poem 'making use of' the tune of say 'L'Alemanda'.

The sonnet was first the 'little tune', the first strophe of a canzone, the form found when some chap got so far and couldn't proceed. Steadily in the wake of the sonneteers came the dull poets.

Arriving by another declivity:
Time and again you will find the statement 'The iambic

was the metre of satire'. And it would seem as if humanity can for centuries read certain perfectly intelligent statements without ingurgitating the *least drop* of their meaning.

The Latin iambic pentameter descends into the modern ten- or eleven-syllable (so-called) 'iambic' pentameter. It is the metre of moral reproof.

It came handy or natural to Pope in a misborn world. Rochester, who had less moral urge, uses it better, mostly because he is used to singing.

There is nothing to be said against moral reform. Born in a town with bad sewers, the man with a good nose will certainly agitate for their improvement. It is not the pleasantest occupation, nor the highest use of human faculties.

But the man who agitates is an infinitely better fellow than the parasite who sabotages the work, or who waits till he can get a percentage on the contract for new cloacae.

There is something to be said against moral fervour that damages music. It is probably a fervour based on imperfect ethics, or on ethics not truly understood. Confucius saw something better and believed that the nastiness in a man's character would damage his music.

Ineluctably song clarifies writing as long as they stick together. It forces the listener to attend to the words, if only by repetition, that is until you get to the last deliquescence, where the musician, despairing, possibly, of finding an intelligent author, abandons the words altogether, and uses inarticulate sound.

This occurs in modern opera. The fact that there is a printed libretto, means nothing.

The writing may be on paper, but it is not *used* by the musician. The words aren't set. If examined they usually have no interest. The musician would probably be unable to set any words that had an interest. You wallow with Puccini and Giordano, etc. . . .

In a decent period you find: Qui perd ses mots perd son ton, as an axiom. Who loses his words loses his note.

While on the subject of Rochester's technique, the student can by inspection of the complete text consider how little or how much has since been added. A great deal that Yeats has painfully worked out, he might have found there already. The best part of Heine's technique is anticipated by Rochester and Dorset. It would surprise me greatly if FitzGerald had not read the address to Nothing, and indeed the whole of our poet. Ingenious comparers can enjoy themselves on the problem:

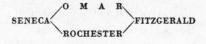

. . . . .

As if Divinity had catched
The itch in order to be scratch'd,
Or like a mountebank did wound
And stab himself with doubts profound
Only to show with how small pain
The sores of Faith are cured again,
Although by woful proof we find
They always leave a scar behind.
He knew the seat of Paradise,
Could tell in what degree it lies
And, as he was dispos'd, could prove it
Below the moon or else above it:
What Adam dreamt of when his bride
Came from her closet in his side,
Whether the devil tempted her
By an High-Dutch[1] interpreter,
If either of them had a navel,
Who first made music malleable[2]
Whether the serpent, at the fall
Had cloven feet or none at all,
All this without a gloss or comment
He could unriddle in a moment
In proper terms such as men smatter
When they throw out and miss the matter.
      For his religion, it was fit
To match his learning and his wit,
'Twas Presbyterian true blue
For he was of that stubborn crew

[1] reference to Becanus' theory of antiquity of Teutonic language
[2] Pythagoras hearing blacksmith

Of errant saints whom all men grant
To be the true church militant
Such as do build their faith upon
The holy text of pike and gun;
Decide all controversy by
Infallible artillery,
And prove their doctrine orthodox
By apostolic blows and knocks;
Call fire sword and desolation
A godly-thorough reformation
Which always must be carried on,
And still is doing but never done,
As if Religion were intended
For nothing else but being mended.
A sect whose chief devotion lies
In odd perverse antipathies,
In falling out with that and this
And finding somewhat still amiss,
More peevish, cross and splenetic
Than dog distract or monkey sick
That with more care keep holy-day
The wrong, than others the right way.[1]
Compound for sins they are inclin'd to
By damning those they have no mind to,
Still so perverse and opposite
As if they worshipp'd God for spite.

Technique of satiric burlesque already at its best, W. N.'s
introductory note to the edition of 1835, remarks: 'a
mirrour in which an Englishman might have seen his face

[1] Xmas fast ordered in 1645. Banquet to Cromwell on Ash Wednesday

161

without becoming, Narcissus-like, enamoured of it'. Butler's eight-syllable verse has been followed but never surpassed either by Pope's ten-syllable couplet or by Byron's strophe form in Don Juan. The fun of rhymes enjoyed by Butler, Dorset, and Rochester attains its known maximum unless it be for Tom Hood's firecracker crackle in Kilmansegg. Gilbert and Sullivan invent nothing that isn't already there (metrically) in a poem like Dorset's

> To all you ladies now on land
> We men at sea indite.

Butler was the son of a churchwarden. His best editor was the Rev. T. R. Nash, D.D. In what I take to be Nash's note on Bk. I, l. 64, the reading of the first edition is added in italics with the remark: 'Many vulgar, and some indecent phrases, were afterward corrected by Mr. Butler. And indeed, as Mr. Cowley observes

> 'tis just
> The author blush, there where his reader must.'

The Rev. N. leaves us our choice.

Whate'er men speak by this new light,
Still they are sure to be i' th' right,
'Tis a dark lanthorn of the spirit,
Which none see by but those that bear it.

Puritan twang burlesqued. The American New England dialect and many other forms of so-called American accent, are accents of different English counties and districts. The *i* like a very short *e* 'speret'.

A light that falls down from on high
For spiritual trades to cozen by,
An ignis fatuus that bewitches
And leads men into pools and ditches
To make them dip themselves and sound
For Christendom in dirty pond,
To dive like wild-fowl for salvation
And fish to catch regeneration.[1]

[1] Recent case of man selling old lottery tickets to African natives at five shillings each, assuring them they were railway tickets to heaven

---

The trouble with this kind of verse as *reading matter* comes from the fact that the fun of comic rhyming leads the author into repetitions and into introducing unnecessary matter. Then again, in the long run human intelligence is more interesting, and more mysterious than human stupidity, and stays new for longer.

Synods are mystical bear-gardens
Where elders, deputies, church-wardens
And other members of the court
Manage the Babylonish sport
For prolocutor, scribe and bearward
Do differ only in a mere word,
Both are but several synagogues
Of carnal men, and bears, and dogs,
. . . . .

The one with men, the other beasts,
The diff'rence is, the one fights with
The tongue, the other with the teeth

. . . . .

Expos'd to scribes and presbyters
Instead of mastiff dogs and curs
Than whom they've less humanity.

. . . . .

What makes morality a crime,
The most notorious of our time;
Morality, which both the saints
And wicked too, cry out against?

. . . . .

'Tis to restore, with more security,
Rebellion to its ancient purity,
And Christian liberty reduce

To th' elder practice of the Jews,
For a large conscience is all one
And signifies the same with none.

The unexpectedness of even a very good joke is bound to wear off on the fifth or sixth reading. The humour of Hermes' remark to Calypso is always there, perfectly solid: 'You a Goddess, ask of me who am a God, nevertheless I will tell you the truth.'

The humour of Butler and of Pope wears off in just the measure that it is 'abstract', general statement or comment, and not particular presentation.

The *root* weakness of eighteenth-century literature will I think be found in the failure to make this fundamental dissociation of ideas.

'Tis hard to say, if greater want of skill
Appear in writing or in judging ill,
But of the two, less dangerous is the offence
To tire the patience than mislead the sense.

. . . . .

Let such teach others as themselves excell

. . . . .

Nature affords at least a glimmering light

. . . . .

So by false learning is good sense defaced
Some are bewildered in a maze of schools
And some made coxcombs nature meant but fools.

Some have at first for wits, then poets passed,
Turn'd critics next, and proved plain fools at last.

. . . . .

Pride, malice, folly, against Dryden rose
˙In various shapes of parsons, critics, beaux:

. . . . .

To err is human, to forgive, divine.

. . . . .

Jilts ruled the state and statesmen farces writ,
Nay wits had pensions and young lords had wit.

Comment, abstract statement, the metre is really too
easy. There is almost no particular statement. The texture
of the lines is seen to be prose texture as soon as the
rhyme dazzle is removed. It is called 'Pope's polished
verse', but compare it to the Donne already given.

There are scores of lines in Pope that hundreds of people can quote, each person meaning thereby something different, or something so vague and general that it has almost no meaning whatever.

The age of politics.

In the lines cited Pope comes nearest to being admirable in his mention of Dryden, where his statement of the situation is correct, but when he says

And such as Chaucer is, shall Dryden be

the statement simply isn't so, and the habitual expresser of opinion is seen to have opinion itself as his contents. I mean as distinct from Chaucerian knowledge of men or Donne's knowledge of what had been at least thoroughly thought.

Note that for all its 'finish' if you try to read a full page of the couplets, you will find many unnecessary words, and a continual tendency to repetition of statements already quite clear or obvious.

His grip is firmer in the Dunciad.

The mighty mother, and her son who brings
The Smithfield muses to the ear of kings,
I sing.   . . . . .
In eldest times e'er mortals writ or read,
Ere Pallas issued from the Thunderer's head,
Dulness o'er all possessed her ancient right,
Daughter of Chaos and eternal night,
Fate in their dotage this fair idiot gave
Gross as her sire, and as her mother grave,
Laborious, heavy, busy, bold and blind,
She ruled in native anarchy the mind.

                              . . . . .

Great Cibber's brazen brainless brothers stand

                    . . . . .

Sepulchral lies our holy walls to grace

A great deal has been written about Pope's bitterness
in attack, by people who neglect to note, or at any rate
neglect to mention, that these attacks coincided with expressions of respect to the better authors (as Dryden and
Swift for example) whom he attempts to weed out from
writers who were nuisances in his day and who are now
so forgotten that his work needs footnotes longer than the
text itself.

How here he sipped, how here he plundered snug
And sucked all o'er like an industrious bug.
Here lay poor Fletcher's half-eat scenes, and here
The frippery of crucified Moliere.
There hapless Shakespeare, yet of Tibbald[1] sore
Wish'd he had blotted for himself before.

. . . . .

Prose swelled to verse, verse loitering into prose,
How random thoughts now meaning chance to find,
Now leave all memory of sense behind,
How prologues into prefaces decay,
And these to notes are frittered quite away,
How index-learning turns no student pale,
Yet holds the eel of science by the tail,
    How with less reading than makes felons 'scape,
Less human genius than God gives an ape,
Small thanks to France, and none to Rome or
    Greece . . . . .
A past, vamp'd, future, old, revived, new piece
Twixt Plautus, Fletcher, Shakespeare and Corneille
Can make a Cibber, Tibbald or Ozell.

[1] an editor

Definite criticism, at least in Pope's mind. The Dunciad
in large chunks is very hard reading simply because we
have the very greatest possible difficulty in beating up
ANY interest whatever in the bores he is writing about.
Even if one does remember a particularly lively crack it is

almost too much trouble to find it again (confession of present author, looking for a few lines he would like to quote). Nevertheless, Pope should be given credit for his effort at drainage.

He is constantly fishing out the better writers. Sic Dunciad II, 124: Congreve, Addison and Prior. 127: Gay, sieved out from seven authors now completely forgotten.

DUNCIAD 1726

A decent priest where monkeys were the gods.
. . . . .

Gay dies unpensioned with a hundred friends.
. . . . .

Book II, along about l. 270, gets up a momentum and I find it possible to run on for a while without skipping. But I am a specialist getting on toward my fiftieth year, with a particular and matured interest in writing and even in literary criticism. I think it would be sheer idiocy to try to force this kind of reading on the general reader, and nothing could dry up the interest of a young student more quickly than telling him he must, should, or ought to BE INTERESTED in such pages. Such reading is not even training for writers. It is a specialized form of archaeology.

The root of the dullness is in the fact that a good deal of Pope isn't informative! We don't really know anything more about his gilded bug that stinks and stings after

reading of him, than we did before. We do get a few points
on the state of scholarship, journalism, etc. . . .

'Give up Cicero to C or K'
. . . . .

Hibernian politics, O Swift, thy fate!
And Pope's, ten years to comment and translate.
. . . . .

Perfectly lucid estimate but almost prophetic anticipa-
tion in:

Proceed, great days, till learning fly the shore,
Till birch shall blush with noble blood no more,
Till Thames see Eton's sons for ever play

When my young Master's Worship comes to Town,
From Pedagogue, and Mother, just set free;
The Heir and Hopes of a great Family:
Who with strong Beer, and Beef, the Country rules;
And ever since the Conquest, have been Fools:
And now, with careful prospect to maintain
This Character, lest crossing of the Strain
Shou'd mend the Booby-breed; his Friends provide
A Cousin of his own to be his Bride:

By Rochester. From 'A Letter from Artemisa in the
Town to Chloe in the Country'. Rochester 1638–1680
                              Pope 1688–1744
Rochester's poem contains also the lines:

Dear Artemisa! Poetry's a Snare
Bedlam has many Mansions: have a care:
Your Muse diverts you, makes the Reader sad:

Observe that Hudibras, Pope, even Crabbe all take us to
a DATED world, to a past state of England. Rochester is
London, 1914. Not only by the modernity of his language
but by his whole disposition (Anschauung) or 'point of
view'.

Pope's heaviness may quite well be due to his desire for
uplift, due ultimately to economic strain, or say that under
the Dunciad is his desire for a specific improvement of a
condition, a dissociation of two grades of writing, whereas
Rochester is free of specific social urge, and his eye lights
on the eternal silliness, persisting after the problem of
leisure has been solved.

Sequence of authors through whom the metamorphosis of English verse writing may be traced.

Chaucer	1340–1400
Villon	1431–sometime after 1465
Gavin Douglas	1474–1522
Golding	1536–1605
Marlowe	1564–93
Shakespeare	1564–1616
Mark Alex. Boyd	1563–1601
John Donne	1573–1631
Thos. Campion	1567?–1619
Robt. Herrick	1591–1674
Waller	1606–87
Sam. Butler	1612–80
Earl of Dorset	1638–1706
Rochester	1647–80
Pope	1688–1744
Crabbe	1754–1832
Landor	1775–1864
Browning	1812–89
FitzGerald	1809–83
Walt Whitman	1819–92
Théo. Gautier	1811–72
Corbière	1840–75
Rimbaud	1854–91
Laforgue	1860–87

It is not the teacher's place to enforce an opinion. The best he can do for himself or his pupil is to take certain simple precautions or to put the pupil in position to take them. For example, it is unwise to estimate a given author or period without looking at, *at least*, some work of the period just precedent; thus before coming to an absolute fixation about 'the eighteen nineties', look at a little Rossetti, before deciding about Rossetti, read a few pages of Browning, and thence in like manner.

The good writers suffer nothing whatever from such comparisons. A critic's ignorance is apt to lie cruelly open if he refuse to make such experiments, or neglect to make fair inspection.

Distinguish clearly between the two sorts of reagent

A. Work of the period or decade just precedent.
B. Work of a remote period, so different that it may show up none of the faults very clearly.

Bad poetry is the same in all languages. What the Chinese call rice-powder poetry differs very little from what was called in Europe 'l'art de Pétrarquiser'.

The nearer you approach the amoeba the less difference in organization.

To what famed college we our vicar owe,
To what fair county, let historians show:
Few now remember when the mild young man,
Ruddy and fair, his Sunday task began;
Few live to speak of that soft soothing look
He cast around, as he prepared his book;
It was a kind of supplicating smile,
But nothing hopeless of applause, the while;
And when he finished, his corrected pride
Felt the desert, and yet the praise denied.

Thus he his race began, and to the end
His constant care was, no man to offend;
No haughty virtues stirr'd his peaceful mind,
Nor urged the priest to leave the flock behind;
He was his Master's soldier, but not one
To lead an army of his martyrs on:
Fear was his ruling passion: yet was love,
Of timid kind, once known his heart to move;
It led his patient spirit where it paid
Its languid offerings to a listening maid;
She, with her widow'd mother, heard him speak,
And sought a while to find what he would seek:
Smiling he came, he smiled when he withdrew,
And paid the same attention to the two;
Meeting and parting without joy or pain,
He seem'd to come that he might go again.

Presentation, description, in place of Popean comment.

CRABBE'S *The Borough*, 1810

Lo! yonder shed; observe its garden-ground,
With the low paling, form'd of wreck, around:
There dwells a fisher; if you view his boat,
With bed and barrel 't is his house afloat;
Look at his house, where ropes, nets, blocks, abound,
Tar, pitch, and oakum—'t is his boat aground:
That space enclosed, but little he regards,
Spread o'er with relics of masts, sails, and yards:
Fish by the wall, on spit of elder, rest,
Of all his food, the cheapest and the best,
By his own labour caught, for his own hunger dress'd.

Here our reformers come not; none object
To paths polluted, or upbraid neglect;
None care that ashy heaps at doors are cast,
That coal-dust flies along the blinding blast:
None heed the stagnant pools on either side,
Where new-launch'd ships of infant sailors ride:
Rodneys in rags here British valour boast,
And lisping Nelsons fright the Gallic coast.
They fix the rudder, set the swelling sail,
They point the bowsprit and they blow the gale:
True to her port the frigate scuds away,

Change from Pope to Crabbe, change from Voltaire to
Stendhal and Flaubert. Crabbe conveying information, not
yet eschewing comment on principle, though much more
effective where he doesn't insert it.

Perfectly clear even from these two excerpts that he is

doing the novelist's work, Dickens, Disraeli, etc. History of the state of England at the start of the nineteenth century, Michelet's method already in use.

> That window view!—oil'd paper and old glass
> Stain the strong rays, which, though impeded, pass
> And give a dusty warmth to that huge room,
>
> . . . . .
>
> Pale and faint upon the floor they fall
> Or feebly gleam on the opposing wall,
> The floor, once oak, now piec'd with fir unplaned

Crabbe's dates 1754 to 1832—Jane Austen's 1775 to 1817.

But *The Borough* did not appear till 1810. It would be far easier to counterfeit Crabbe's poem than to write a Jane Austen novel.

And these novels are, with perfect justice, the more widely read a century after Crabbe's death. Crabbe is undeniably reading matter, not singing matter, and he is well worth reading though I don't imagine he is greatly re-read. Jane's novels don't either replace him or wipe him from the map. Rhymed couplets are unlikely to compete with De Maupassant, let alone with Hollywood.

If one is convinced that the film offers, in the present century, a better form than the stage, he is unlikely to advise anyone to write any *more* rhymed couplets.

On the other hand, given a curiosity about the social condition of England in 1810, can you find a more condensed account than Crabbe's of the whole social order?

The British novelists' dates are (for comparison)
Richardson 1689–1761
Fielding 1707–54
Smollett 1721–71
Sterne 1713–68

Reading Crabbe is a bit like trying to go somewhere on Fulton's first steamboat; he does, nevertheless, get you somewhere, and on the whole if you compare him with English prose fiction of an earlier date, his verse is as readable as anything save possibly the first part of *Tom Jones*, Sterne's *Sentimental Journey*, and *Tristram Shandy* as far as that interminable sermon wherein many readers must afore now have been boggit.

The Rev. Crabbe had, by contrast to Landor, no Greek, as he tells us in 'The Borough' (Prison).

> Homer, nay Pope! (for never will I seek
> Applause for learning—naught have I with Greek)
> Gives us the secrets of his pagan hell
> Where ghost with ghost in sad communion dwell
>
> . . . . .
>
> When a new spirit in that world was found
> A thousand shadowy forms came flitting round

But his early medical training came in handy at least once when he was visiting a country house and the midwife failed to arrive. . . . Landor would not in such case have been of signal assistance.

The child was called Lemuel in reference to intervention if not of heaven, at least to an ordained subaltern.

From Alcaeus

Wormwood and rue be on his tongue
    And ashes on his head,
Who chills the feast and checks the song
    With emblems of the dead!

Be young and jovial, wise and brave,
    Such mummers are derided.
His sacred rites shall Bacchus have
    Unspared and undivided.

Caught by my friends, I fear no mask
    Impending from above,
I only fear the latter flask
    That holds me from my love.

LANDOR 1775–1864

Epithalamium

Weep Venus and ye
Adorable Three
Who Venus for ever environ.
Pounds, shillings and pence
And shrewd sober sense
Have clapt the strait waistcoat on * * *

Asterisks left by the author and concealing nothing.
179

Off Lainot and Turk
With pistol and dirk,
Nor palace nor pinnace set fire on,
The cord's fatal jerk
Has done its last work
And the noose is now slipped upon * * *

Asterisks left by the author and concealing nothing.

CLXXXIV

God's laws declare
Thou shalt not swear
By aught in heaven above or earth below.

Upon my honour! Melville cries;
He swears, and lies;
Does Melville then break God's commandment?
No.

Landor: Poems and Epigrams,
probably edition of 1846

CLXXXIX

Does it become a girl so wise,
So exquisite in harmonies,
To ask me when I do intend
To write a sonnet? What? my friend!
A sonnet? Never. Rhyme o'erflows
Italian, which hath scarcely prose;
And I have larded full three-score
With *sorte, morte, cuor, amor.*

But why should we, altho' we have
Enough for all things, gay or grave,
Say, on your conscience, why should we
Who draw deep seans along the sea,
Cut them in pieces to beset
The shallows with a cabbage-net?
Now if you ever ask again
A thing so troublesome and vain,
By all your charms! before the morn,
To show my anger and my scorn,
First I will write your name a-top,
Then from this very ink shall drop
A score of sonnets; every one
Shall call you star, or moon, or sun,
Till, swallowing such warm-water verse,
Even sonnet-sippers sicken worse.

CCXX

. . . . .

Since Chaucer was alive and hale
No man hath walkt along our roads with step
So active, so enquiring eye, or tongue
So varied in discourse.

But warmer climes
Give brighter plumage, stronger wing: the breeze
Of Alpine heights thou playest with, borne on
Beyond Sorrento and Amalfi, where
The Siren waits thee, singing song for song.

(From his lines to Robt. Browning)

181

The Duke of York's Statue

Enduring is the bust of bronze,
And thine, O flower of George's sons,
Stands high above all laws and duns.

As honest men as ever cart
Convey'd to Tyburn, took thy part
And raised thee up to where thou art.

XIV   From Last Fruit off an old tree

Ireland never was contented . . .
Say you so? you are demented.
Ireland was contented when
All could use the sword and pen,
And when Tara rose so high
That her turrets split the sky,

And about her courts were seen
Liv'ried Angels robed in green,
Wearing, by St. Patrick's bounty,
Emeralds big as half a county.

Macaulay's Peerage

>   Macaulay is become a peer;
>   A coronet he well may wear;
>   But is there no one to malign?
>   None: then his merit wants the sign.

Heroic Idylls with Additional Poems

XIII

>   'Twas far beyond the midnight hour
>   And more than half the stars were falling,
>   And jovial friends, who'd lost the power
>   Of sitting, under chairs lay sprawling;
>
>   Not Porson so; his stronger pate
>   Could carry more of wine and Greek
>   Than Cambridge held; erect he sate;
>   He nodded, yet could somehow speak:
>
>   ''Tis well, O Bacchus! they are gone,
>   Unworthy to approach thy altar!
>   The pious man prays best alone,
>   Nor shall thy servant falter.'
>
>   Then Bacchus too, like Porson, nodded.
>   Shaking the ivy on his brow,
>   And graciously replied the godhead:
>   'I have no votary staunch as thou.'

183

Past ruin'd Ilion Helen lives
 Alcestis rises from the Shades;
Verse calls them forth; 'tis Verse that gives
 Immortal Youth to mortal Maids.

Soon shall Oblivion's deepening Veil
 Hide all the peopled Hills ye see,
The gay, the proud, while Lovers hail
 These many summers you and me.

The tear for fading Beauty check
 For passing Glory cease to sigh,
One Form shall rise above the Wreck,
 One name, *Ianthe*, shall not die.

Old Style

Aurelius, Sire of Hungrinesses!
Thee thy old friend Catullus blesses,
And sends thee six fine watercresses.
There are those who would not think me quite
(Unless we were old friends) polite
To mention whom you should invite.
Look at them well; and turn it o'er
In your own mind . . . I'd have but four . . .
Lucullus, Caesar, and two more.

Landor, the man of letters, usually invoked as model of the 'lapidary style' or of the 'well-turned verse'. The effect of his severe classical studies never deserts him, and the cantabile quality never wholly deserts the verses of his shorter poems, even when they are manifestly *inscribed*.

DIRCE

Stand close around, ye Stygian set
With Dirce in one bark convey'd,
Or Charon seeing, may forget
That he is old, and she a shade.

Moral: a man wanting to conserve a tradition would always do well to find out, first, what it is.

A man preferring 'a manner of writing' to the living language, runs considerable danger if he have not a culture as thorough as Landor's, and a great part of Landor's longer poems are still inaccessible because the language is so far removed from any speech ever used anywhere.

You go to Crabbe for England of 1810, you can go to Landor for an epitome; all culture of the encyclopedists reduced to manageable size, in the *Imaginary Conversations* and full of human life ventilated, given a human body, not merely indexed.

A figure to put against Voltaire. BUT for the Chronology! Voltaire was at WORK shovelling out the garbage, the Bourbons, the really filthy decayed state of French social thought.

Voltaire: 1694–1778.

Landor: 1775–1864

They are mental contemporaries. Landor comes after the work is done, Rabelais, Peter Bayle, Voltaire, Diderot, Holbach, or further back Bude, Lorenzo Valla, Landor gathers it up, and if you want a handy introduction you have it in his *Conversations*; written in Stendhal's time (1783–1842).

Voltaire's English contemporary was chronologically Samuel Johnson (1709–84) listed as 'moralist, essayist and lexicographer', a figure of fun, an absurdity, the stage Englishman of Goldoni, 1707–93, admirable because he will not lick boots, but intellectually 'fuori del mondo', living in the seventeenth century, so far as Europe is concerned.

Very possibly the best mind in England of his day, save for those months that Voltaire spent in London.

. . . . .

Landor's Dialogues are richer than Fontenelle's, but Fontenelle was born in 1657 and died in 1757.

Landor's addition differs from that which Chaucer infused into his continental matter, but the parallel is worth inspecting. In Landor's case the time lag must be computed. He was so far ahead of his British times that the country couldn't contain him, and Anatole France was still in a certain sense going on in wake of Landor, within living memory, and indeed down to the day of his death, a man of much slighter importance.

TO RECAPITULATE

CHAUCER contemporary, participant in the continental life of his time, in the mind of the continent, though his technique was in part centuries old.

SHAKESPEARE (Jacques Père, spelling it Shaxpear, because J is either pronounced hard or confused with I) making sixteenth-century plays out of fifteenth-century Italian news. The Italian stage had given the commedia dell' arte, and Italian oratory, law court stuff, the example of ornate speeches. Shakespeare already looking back to Europe from the outside.

LANDOR 80 per cent retrospective, though this mustn't be taken to mean that he wasn't driving piles into the mud, and preparing foundations—which have been largely unused by his successors.

In Mantua territory half is slough,
Half pine-tree forest, maples, scarlet oaks
Breed o'er the river-beds, even Mincio
    chokes
With sand the summer through, but 'tis
    morass
In winter up to Mantua walls. There
    was,
Some thirty years before this evening's
    coil,
One spot reclaimed from the surrounding
    spoil;
Goito, just a castle built amid
A few low mountains; firs and larches
    hid
Their main defiles and rings of vineyard
    bound
The rest . . . . .

You gain the inmost chambers, gain at
    last
A maple-panelled room; that haze which
    seems
Floating about the panel if there gleams
A sunbeam over it, will turn to gold
And in light-graven characters unfold
The Arab's wisdom everywhere; what
    shade
Marred them a moment, those slim pillars
    made,

Cut like a company of palms to prop
The roof, each kissing top entwined with
    top,
Leaning together; in the carver's mind
Some knot of bacchanals, flushed cheek
    combined
With straining forehead, shoulders purpled,
    hair
Diffused between, who in a goat skin bear
A vintage; graceful sister-palms! But
    quick
To the main wonder, now. A vault,
    see; thick
Black shade about the ceiling, though
    fine slits
Across the buttress suffer light by fits
Upon a marvel in the midst. Nay,
    stoop—
A dullish grey-streaked cumbrous font, a
    group
Round it—each side of it, where'er one
    sees—
Upholds it; shrinking Caryatides
Of just-tinged marble like Eve's lillied
    flesh
Beneath her maker's finger when the fresh
First pulse of life shot brightening the
    snow,
The font's edge burthens every shoulder, so
They muse upon the ground, eyelids half
    closed,

189

Some, with meek arms behind their backs
    disposed,
Some, crossed above their bosoms, some,
    to veil
Their eyes, some, propping chin and cheek
    so pale,
Some, hanging slack an utter helpless
    length
Dead as a buried vestal whose whole
    strength
Goes, when the grate above shuts heavily,
So dwell these noiseless girls, patient to see
Like priestesses because of sin impure
Penanced forever, who resigned endure,
Having that once drunk sweetness to the
    dregs.
And every eve, Sordello's visit begs
Pardon for them; constant at eve he
    came
To sit beside each in her turn, the same
As one of them, a certain space; and
    awe
Made a great indistinctness till he saw
Sunset slant cheerful through the buttress-
    chinks,
Gold seven times globed; surely our
    maiden shrinks
And a smile stirs her as if one faint
    grain
Her load were lightened, one shade less
    the stain

Obscured her forehead, yet one more bead
    slipt
From off the rosary whereby the crypt
Keeps count of the contritions of its
    charge?

ROBT. BROWNING 1812–89

Victorian half-wits claimed that this poem was obscure, and the predecessors of Z, Y, X, Q.N and company used to pride themselves on grinning through the horse-collar: 'Only two lines of Sordello were intelligible.'

As Renan has remarked, 'Il n'y a que la bêtise humaine qui donne une idée de l'infini'.

Browning had attained this limpidity of narration and published Sordello at the age of 28 (A.D. 1840).

There is here a certain lucidity of sound that I think you will find with difficulty elsewhere in English, and you very well may have to retire as far as the Divina Commedia for continued narrative having such clarity of outline without clog and *verbal* impediment.

It will be seen that the author is telling you something, not merely making a noise, he does not gum up the sound. The 'beauty' is not applied ornament, but makes the mental image more definite. The author is not hunting about for large high-sounding words, there is a very great variety in the rhyme but the reader runs on unaware.

Again as in the case of Golding, the reader must read it as prose, pausing for the sense and not hammering the line-terminations.

WHITMAN

From an examination of Walt made twelve years ago the
present writer carried away the impression that there are
thirty well-written pages of Whitman; he is now unable to
find them. Whitman's faults are superficial, he does convey
an image of his time, he has written histoire morale, as
Montaigne wrote the history of his epoch. You can learn
more of nineteenth-century America from Whitman than
from any of the writers who either refrained from perceiving, or limited their record to what they had been
taught to consider suitable literary expression. The only
way to enjoy Whitman thoroughly is to concentrate on his
fundamental meaning. If you insist, however, on dissecting
his language you will probably find that it is wrong NOT
because he broke all of what were considered in his day
'the rules' but because he is spasmodically conforming to
this, that or the other; sporadically dragging in a bit of
'regular' metre, using a bit of literary language, and
putting his adjectives where, in the spoken tongue, they
are not. His real writing occurs when he gets free of all this
barbed wire.

Certainly the last author to be tried in a classroom.

In the main I don't see that teaching can do much more
than expose counterfeit work, thus gradually leading the
student to the valid. The hoax, the sham, the falsification
become so habitual that they pass unnoticed; all this is fit
matter for education. The student can in this field profit by
his instructor's experience. The natural destructivity of

the young can function to advantage: excitement of the chase, the fun of detection could under favourable circumstance enliven the study.

Whereas it is only maturer patience that can sweep aside a writer's honest error, and overlook unaccomplished clumsiness or outlandishness or old-fashionedness, for the sake of the solid centre.

Thus many clever people have overlooked Thomas Hardy's verses, even though the author of the *Mayor of Casterbridge* lurks behind them.

Narrative sense, narrative power can survive ANY truncation. If a man have the tale to tell and can keep his mind on that and refuses to worry about his own limitations, the reader will, in the long or short run, find him, and no amount of professorial abuse or theoretical sniping will have any real effect on the author's civil status. Barrels of ink have flowed to accuse Mr. Kipling of vulgarity (that was perhaps before the present reader was born), to accuse him of being a journalist . . . etc. . . . .

Thomas Hardy's Noble Dames and Little Ironies will find readers despite all the French theories in the world.

More writers fail from lack of character than from lack of intelligence.

Technical solidity is not attained without at least some persistence.

The chief cause of false writing is economic. Many writers

need or want money. These writers could be cured by an application of banknotes.

The next cause is the desire men have to tell what they don't know, or to pass off an emptiness for a fullness. They are discontented with what they have to say and want to make a pint of comprehension fill up a gallon of verbiage.

An author having a very small amount of true contents can make it the basis of formal and durable mastery, provided he neither inflates nor falsifies: Vide the Aucassin, the Canzoni of Arnaut, the Daphnis and Chloe.

The plenum of letters is not bounded by primaeval exclusivity functioning against any *kind* of human being or talent, but only against false coiners, men who will not dip their metal in the acid of known or accessible fact.

TREATISE ON METRE

I

I HEARD a fair lady sigh: 'I wish someone would write a good treatise on prosody.'

As she had been a famous actress of Ibsen, this was not simple dilettantism, but the sincere wish for something whereof the lack had been inconvenient. Apart from Dante's *De Vulgari Eloquio* I have encountered only one treatise on metric which has the slightest value. It is Italian and out of print, and has no sort of celebrity.

The confusion in the public mind has a very simple cause: the desire to get something for nothing or to learn an art without labour.

Fortunately or unfortunately, people CAN write stuff that passes for poetry, before they have studied music.

The question is extremely simple. Part of what a musician HAS to know is employed in writing with words; there are no special 'laws' or 'differences' in respect to *that part*. There is a great laxity or vagueness permitted the poet in regard to *pitch*. He may be as great a poet as Mr. Yeats and still think he doesn't know one note from another.

Mr. Yeats probably would distinguish between a *g* and a *b flat*, but he is happy to think that he doesn't, and he would certainly be incapable of whistling a simple melody in tune.

197

Nevertheless before writing a lyric he is apt to 'get a chune[1] in his head'.

He is very sensitive to a limited gamut of rhythms.

Rhythm is a form cut into TIME, as a design is determined SPACE.

A melody is a rhythm in which the pitch of each element is fixed by the composer.

(Pitch: the number of vibrations per second.)

I said to a brilliant composer[2] and pupil of Kodaly:

These people can't make a melody, they can't make a melody four bars long.

He roared in reply: Four bars, they can't make one TWO bars long!

Music is so badly taught that I don't suggest every intending poet should bury himself in a conservatory. The *Laurencie et Lavignac Encycléopdie de la Musique et Dictionnaire du Conservatoire*'[3] has however an excellent section on Greek metric, better than one is likely to find in use in the Greek language department of your university.

In making a line of verse (and thence building the lines into passages) you have certain primal elements:

That is to say, you have the various 'articulate sounds' of the language, of its alphabet, that is, and the various groups of letters in syllables.

---

[1] *ch*, Neo-Celtic for *t*   [2] Tibor Serly
[3] Pub. Delagrave, Paris

198

These syllables have differing weights and durations

A. original weights and durations
B. weights and durations that seem naturally imposed on them by the other syllable groups around them.

Those are the medium wherewith the poet cuts his design in TIME.

If he hasn't a sense of time and of the different qualities of sound, this design will be clumsy and uninteresting just as a bad draughtsman's drawing will be without distinction.

The bad draughtsman is bad because he does not perceive space and spatial relations, and cannot therefore deal with them.

The writer of bad verse is a bore because he does not perceive time and time relations, and cannot therefore delimit them in an interesting manner, by means of longer and shorter, heavier and lighter syllables, and the varying qualities of sound inseparable from the words of his speech.

He expects his faculty to descend from heaven? He expects to train and control that faculty without the labour that even a mediocre musician expends on qualifying to play fourth tin horn in an orchestra, and the result is often, and quite justly, disesteemed by serious members of his profession.

Symmetry or strophic forms naturally HAPPENED in lyric poetry when a man was singing a long poem to a short

199

melody which he had to use over and over. There is no particular voodoo or sacrosanctity about symmetry. It is one of many devices, expedient sometimes, advantageous sometimes for certain effects.

It is hard to tell whether music has suffered more by being taught than has verse-writing from having no teachers. Music in the past century of shame and human degradation slumped in large quantities down into a soggy mass of tone.

In general we may say that the deliquescence of instruction in any art proceeds in this manner.

I A master invents a gadget, or procedure to perform a particular function, or a limited set of functions.

Pupils adopt the gadget. Most of them use it less skilfully than the master. The next genius may improve it, or he may cast it aside for something more suited to his own aims.

II Then comes the paste-headed pedagogue or theorist and proclaims the gadget a law, or rule.

III Then a bureaucracy is endowed, and the pin-headed secretariat attacks every new genius and every form of inventiveness for not obeying the law, and for perceiving something the secretariat does not.

The great savants ignore, quite often, the idiocies of the ruck of the teaching profession. Friedrich Richter can

200

proclaim that the rules of counterpoint and harmony have nothing to do with composition, Sauzay can throw up his hands and say that when Bach composed he appears to have done so by a series of 'procedures' whereof the secret escapes us, the hard sense of the one, and not altogether pathetic despair of the other have no appreciable effect on the ten thousand calves led up for the yearly stuffing.

Most arts attain their effects by using a fixed element and a variable.

From the empiric angle: verse usually has some element roughly fixed and some other that varies, but which element is to be fixed and which vary, and to what degree, is the affair of the author.

Some poets have chosen the bump, as the boundary.

Some have chosen to mark out their course with repetition of consonants; some with similar terminations of words. All this is a matter of detail. You can make a purely empiric list of successful manœuvres, you can compile a catalogue of your favourite poems. But you cannot hand out a receipt for making a Mozartian melody on the basis of take a crotchet, then a quaver, then a semi-quaver, etc. . . .

You don't ask an art instructor to give you a recipe for making a Leonardo da Vinci drawing.

Hence the extreme boredom caused by the usual professorial documentation or the aspiring thesis on prosody.

The answer is:

LISTEN to the sound that it makes.

II

THE reader who has understood the first part of this chapter has no need of reading the second. Nothing is more boring than an account of errors one has not committed.

Rhythm is a form cut into time.

. . . . .

The perception that the mind, either of an individual or a nation can decay, and give off all the displeasing vapours of decomposition has unfortunately gone into desuetude. Dante's hell was of those who had lost the increment of intelligence with the capital. Shakespeare, already refining the tough old catholic concept, refers to ignorance merely as darkness.

From the time Thos. Jefferson jotted down an amateur's notes on what seemed to be the current practice of English versification, the general knowledge, especially among hacks, appears to have diminished to zero, and to have passed into infinite negative. I suppose the known maxima occurred in the *North American Review* during Col. Harvey's intumescence. During that era when the directing minds and characters in America had reached a cellarage only to be gazed at across the barriers of libel law, the said editorial bureau rebuked some alliterative verse on the grounds that a consonant had been repeated despite Tennyson's warning.

A parallel occurs in a recent professorial censure of Mr. Binyon's Inferno, the censor being, apparently, in utter ignorance of the nature of Italian syllabic verse, which is composed of various syllabic groups, and not merely strung along with a swat on syllables two, four, six, eight, ten of each line.

You would not expect to create a Mozartian melody or a Bach theme by the process of bumping alternate notes, or by merely alternating quavers and crotchets.

Great obfuscation spread from the failure to dissociate heavy accent and duration.

Other professors failed to comprehend the 'regularity' of classic hexameter.

So called dactylic hexameter does NOT start from ONE type of verse.

There are, mathematically, sixty-four basic general forms of it; of which twenty or thirty were probably found to be of most general use, and several of which would probably have been stunts or rarities.

But this takes no count either of shifting caesura (pause at some point in the line), nor does it count any of the various shadings.

It ought to be clear that the variety starting FROM a colony of sixty-four different general rhythm shapes, or archetypes, will be vastly more compendious, will naturally accommodate a vastly greater amount of real speech, than will a set of variants starting from a single type of line, whether measured by duration or by the alternating heaviness of syllables,

specifically:
ti tum ti tum ti tum ti tum ti tum
203

from which every departure is treated as an exception.

The legal number of syllables in a classic hexameter varied from twelve to eighteen.

When the Greek dramatists developed or proceeded from anterior Greek prosody, they arrived at chorus forms which are to all extents 'free', though a superstructure of nomenclature has been gummed on to them by analysers whom neither Aeschylus nor Euripides would ever have bothered to read.

These nomenclatures were probably invented by people who had never LISTENED to verse, and who probably wouldn't have been able to distinguish Dante's movement from Milton's had they heard it read out aloud.

I believe Shakespeare's 'blank verse' runs from ten to seventeen syllables, but have no intention of trying to count it again, or make a census.

None of these professorial pint pots has anything to do with the question.

Homer did not start by thinking which of the sixty-four permitted formulae was to be used in his next verse.

THE STROPHE

THE reason for strophic form has already been stated. The mediaeval tune, obviously, demanded an approximately even number of syllables in each strophe, but as the duration of the notes was not strictly marked, the tune itself was probably subject to variation within limits. These limits were in each case established by the auditive precision of the troubadour himself.

In Flaubert's phrase: 'Pige moi le typε!' Find me the guy that will set out with sixty-four general matrices for rhythm and having nothing to say, or more especially nothing germane or kindred to the original urge which created those matrices, and who will therewith utter eternal minstrelsy, or keep the reader awake.

As in the case of Prof. Wubb or whatever his name was, the ignorant of one generation set out to make laws, and gullible children next try to obey them.

III

THE populace loved the man who said 'Look into thine owne hearte and write' or approved Uc St. Circ, or whoever it was who recorded: 'He made songs because he had a will to make songs and not because love moved him thereto. And nobody paid much attention to either him or his poetry.'

All of which is an infinite remove from the superstition that poetry isn't an art, or that prosody isn't an art WITH LAWS.

But like the laws of any art they are not laws to be learnt by rule of thumb. 'La sculpture n'est pas pour les jeunes hommes', said Brancusi. Hokusai and Chaucer have borne similar witness.

Pretended treatises giving recipes for metric are as silly as would be a book giving you measurements for producing a masterpiece à la Botticelli.

Proportion, laws of proportion. Pier della Francesca having thought longer, knew more than painters who have not taken the trouble.

'La section d'or'[1] certainly helped master architects. But you learn painting by eye, not by algebra. Prosody and melody are attained by the listening ear, not by an index of nomenclatures, or by learning that such and such a foot is called spondee. Give your draughtsman sixty-four stencils of 'Botticelli's most usual curves'? And he will make you a masterpiece?

Beyond which we will never recover the art of *writing to be sung* until we begin to pay some attention to the sequence, or scale, of vowels in the line, and of the vowels terminating the group of lines in a series.

[1] Traditions of architectural proportion

Homer
Sappho
Catullus
Ovid
Seafarer
Dante
Guido Cavalcanti
Villon
Ta' Hio
Fielding
Shakespeare Sonnets
Jane Austen
✝ Donne (Ecstasy)
Theophile Gautier (Kenava et Camees)
Corbiere
Rimbaud
Laforgue
Robert Browning
✝ Chaucer
✝ Gavin Douglas (Aeneid)
✝ Golding (Ovid's Metamorphosis)
✝ Marlowe (Amore
✝ Shakespeare (plays & lyrics
✝ Fitzgerald (Rubaiyat)
Herrick
Campion
Waller
Donne
Rochester

Sterne
Trollope
Mark Alexander Boyd

Music note when it get too far from the dance

Poetry atrophies when it gets too far from music